How_T

Claiming
Compensation

Claiming Compensation

How to claim and gain what is due to you

KEITH BROOKS

How To Books

Published by How To Books Ltd,
3 Newtec Place, Magdalen Road,
Oxford OX4 1RE, United Kingdom.
Tel: (01865) 793806. Fax: (01865) 248780.
email: info@howtobooks.co.uk
http://www.howtobooks.co.uk

First edition 2000

British Library Cataloguing in Publication Data.
A catalogue record for this book is available from
the British Library.

Edited by Alison Wilson
Cover design by Shireen Nathoo Design
Cover image by PhotoDisc
Produced for How To Books by Deer Park Productions
Typeset by Kestrel Data, Exeter
Printed and bound by Cromwell Press Ltd, Trowbridge, Wiltshire

NOTE: The material contained in this book is set out in good
faith for general guidance and no liability can be accepted
for loss or expense incurred as a result of relying in particular
circumstances on statements made in the book. Laws and
regulations are complex and liable to change, and readers should
check the current position with the relevant authorities before
making personal arrangements.

Contents

List of Illustrations

Preface

Coping with modern life is hard enough without the strains other people's negligence throws at us. Many people have had an injury caused by somebody else and the person who is accountable is usually very evasive if compensation is sought or even mentioned. Likewise we have all had problems with faulty repairs or have had to return faulty goods to shops where the assistant has been less than helpful. This book will guide you, in plain English, to the laws relating to consumers and through the simple steps needed to make a claim.

This book covers the main points for getting the maximum amount of compensation and has sections on the main aspects of laws relating to shopping, food, animals etc which could give cause for a claim to be made. Each chapter deals with a different environment where claims could occur such as when walking, cycling, dining out, using a car. If anything happens you have easy access to the information you need whilst at the scene or on your return home.

Many people believe the American system of legal action, where they seem to sue anybody for the smallest matter, would be unworkable in other countries. However, legal action is almost always avoidable as long as the correct steps are taken. Nobody likes the thought of appearing in court because they picture a room full of wigs and gavels. However, the modern system of courts is very user-friendly and should not phase anybody. If you have a valid complaint or grounds for compensation the ones who are to blame will realise this. The last thing they will want is to make your claim greater by having to pay both sets of legal costs, plus court costs and any other fines the court feels fit to impose on them.

To enable you to word letters effectively there are sample letters to guide you. Some contain phrases which may sound odd, but these are explained to you in clear English. They will show the recipient that you mean business.

In most situations a photographic record of accident sites or injuries is very useful. I recommend that you purchase a small camera which is easily accessible (chemists have a range of disposable cameras which are very light and compact).

The book is also valuable to tradespersons, shop owners, etc who can discover what level of customer care they should try to achieve and what is legally expected of them.

Keith Brooks

1

Knowing How to Complain

KNOWING WHEN TO COMPLAIN

Before you make a complaint make sure your approach is focused, like a laser. A large voltage light may give a good spread of light yet a small-power laser gives a better focus. In order to complain with any sort of effectiveness your approach needs to be in an ordered and focussed manner. You need to decide:

- what you are complaining about
- why you are complaining about it
- what level of response you are after.

Lodging the initial complaint

Many trivial complaints can be settled orally at the scene. However if this is inappropriate then inform the other prty that they will be hearing from you in writing. Get a name and their respective position to which to send your mail as this will be useful later.

If you decide on this action then you should:

- Speak reasonably slowly at a fair volume.
- Give the other party a fair chance to put the matter right.
- Remain calm at all times.
- Decide in advance what you would like to happen.

DEFINING YOUR GOALS

Before persuing a complaint it is important to decide what action you want as a result. This of course will depend on what you are actually complaining about. If, for example you are complaining about having tripped and fallen over a loose pavement slab, would you be satisfied to see the pavement repaired? Or would you seek financial compensation? Or both?

- How long you are prepared to fight?
- What could your best result be?
- What is the minimum response you would accept?

Putting it in writing

If your attempt at oral settlement is unsuccessful or inappropriate then the next avenue is a written complaint.

- Send all mail by registered or recorded delivery.
- If hand-delivering get member of staff/receptionist to give a receipt.
- Send mail to named person and position in company if possible.
- Never send original documents as they may be 'lost', photo-copies will suffice.

KEEPING RECORDS

The simplest way of keeping records is the preparation of a document pack. The best type is a clip file with a few clear covers. It will help you take a more organised approach, and if the matter needs handing on to a solicitor at a later date then all the required details are listed.

Your document pack should contain the following:

- photographs
- details of any medical help received
- copies of all correspondence
- diary.

Taking photographs

Photographs are useful for personal injuries, particularly for wounds which look bad for a short time but which do not require professional medical treatment. These include cuts, grazes, smallish burns, bruises and so on. It is often useful to place a coin alongside the injury to give an indication of scale. If appropriate also photograph the accident site. Councils have been known to repair loose slabs within a few hours of a stumble.

Including details of medical treatment
If you are seen at a hospital casualty department you should note the name of the doctor who attended you. You may be asked for this information later. If you are given any medication by hospital staff then ask for details, including dosage. If prescribed any medication then keep the empty packets or boxes.

Taking copies of all correspondence
This will consist of copies of any letters, faxes or electronic mail sent or received, details of the outcome of any telephone calls and also a written record of any conversation relating to the initial complaint.

Keeping a diary
If you have suffered a physical injury then keep a record, on a day-to-day basis, of how that injury has affected you. If you have had to take any medication to cope with the injury or pain then note that too. Follow-up letters and telephone calls are much easier if you have a record of your progress.

GETTING TO THE RIGHT PERSON

Companies often play their cards very close to their chest and getting a name out of them can be difficult. The easiest way to find out is via the switchboard operator who should direct you to someone appropriate. Books such as *Who Owns Who, Kellys Manufacturers and Merchants Directory* and *UK Trade Names* may provide you with the information you need. Enquire at your local library.

You should try to ascertain:

- Name of initial contact and their superior.

- Address where person is mostly situated.

- Their position in the company.

- The company's or preferably their own direct fax number or email address.

- It may prove useful to find out their qualification or professional association as these may be contacted to assist you later.

Knowing who to complain to

If you have a problem in a restaurant do not repeat your complaint to the waiter or assistant as they have no responsibility to rectify it. Ask the waiter to fetch the manager. Conversely if your car is returned a day late after a minor repair don't aim your initial complaint at the managing director of the motor company. Your objective should be to get to the person who can take the appropriate level of action.

The advantage of this is to:

- Avoid stress and anger to yourself.

- Show the other party you are not to be trifled with.

- Show that you have a name to mention to their superior if not satisfied.

SUPPORTING YOUR CLAIM/COMPLAINT

The greatest source of reinforcement is witnesses. They are a very useful tool and should not be ignored as it gives your complaint credence. Other sources of support or guidance are:

- Professional bodies of which they are members.

- Your own solicitor (this is covered in more detail in Chapter 10).

- Doctor's report – you should seek to have any injury noted on your medical records as soon as possible.

Specific area where assistance may be sought

Written evidence that the matter was reported to a higher authority can be extremely useful and add significant weight to your claim.

Certain government departments handle different situations. Any problem should be reported as appropriate.

- Environmental Health Department

- Trading Standards Department

- Police, Fire, Ambulance and Coastguard.

They will usually write to you with their findings, which adds credence. An example of this would be a complaint to a restaurant that contaminated food made you ill. If you mention that an uneaten part of the meal is now with the local Environmental Health Office it will support your case.

Areas covered by Environmental Health Officers

A team of officers oversees many areas of public care. They have the power to inflict serious financial damage on the persons they prosecute. If you feel that any of the following relate to your complaint then they may well be worth a call. For example they will:

- Examine food which may be contaminated.

- Examine any foreign body which was located in food.

- Investigate reports on unhygenic cooking areas.

- Control animal disease.

- Investigate the improper dumping of waste.

- Investigate general breaches in trading standards.

- Control noise and air pollution.

- Inspect factories, shops and offices.

- Provide sewage services (as agents for water company).

Areas covered by Trading Standards

This department's officers also have the powers to inflict serious financial damage on the persons they prosecute. If you believe that you have been handled wrongly by a trader they will be of great aid. The court may award you compensation (but you are still free to sue for more). The main areas policed are:

- Checking short weights or measures.

- Investigating misleading pricing.

- False descriptions of goods.

- Breaches of the Sale of Goods Act.

Areas of complaint covered by an ombudsman

There are various ombudsmen whose task is to investigate com-plaints alleging maladministration cases only. The ombudsman is independent and gives an impartial service at no charge and has the same power as a High Court. There is currently a:

- Local Government Ombudsman

- Parliamentary Ombudsman

- Banking Ombudsman

- Insurance Ombudsman

- Pensions Ombudsman

- Building Societies Ombudsman

- Legal Services Ombudsman

- Corporate Estate Agents Ombudsman.

The ombudsman, however, cannot cover certain areas but it may well be worth attracting their influence. If in doubt contact them, they alone decide if a complaint can be investigated, not your council or councillor. They cannot however investigate complaints about:

- Matters already being handled by a court, tribunal or govern-ment minister.

- Unspecific matters involving the general public.

- Personnel matters.

- Internal affairs of schools or colleges.

There is a specific leaflet, with a complaint form, available from your local council, library or Citizens Advice Bureau.

PUTTING YOUR COMPLAINT IN WRITING

Every letter should have a basic layout stating your own details
and those of the person to whom you are writing. Always mention
dates of previous mail sent to them or refer to the date of any
letters you have received from them. Above all you should
always:

- State any reference numbers or invoice numbers of previous
  mail from them.

- State details clearly, in date order, and mention names and
  dates.

- Give a time limit of say 14 or 28 days or you will take the
  matter to their superior.

- State where the incident actually occurred and the date it
  happened on.

- State what level of action you are actually trying to achieve.

See Figure 1 for a sample letter of complaint.

What if there is no response?

You should always expect a written response stating that your
letter is being dealt with. If the person who the mail is destined for
is unavailable you should receive a letter from another person
with equal status.

Sometimes a response may ask for more information. These
should be answered with caution as they are sometimes biased.
Phrases such as 'what actual injuries were sustained?' or 'the vast
majority of our customers are happy with this area of service' seek
to alienate you. It is common practice for large firms to drag their
heels after receiving a claim for personal injury. Delay, they
hope, will weaken your claim, especially if a minor injury has
healed. This is why doctors' reports and photographic evidence
are important. If faced with this type of company take the following action:

- Write again stating you have had no response. Mention that
  you intend to copy both the original letter and this one to their
  superior.

The Manager
Burgertown Restaurant
Soup Street
Tea Town
Pastry County
BUN BAP

Dear Sir

Whilst in your restaurant on the 14th May 200x I was served
by your head waiter, a Mr Soup who then managed to
dislodge an unsuitably supported gateau from the dessert
trolley into my lap. I reported the matter to your assistant
manager, Mr Bacon, who noted the details in your accident
book.

The suit I was wearing was taken to the cleaners and they
tried to remove the stain but could not do so. In light of this
I am claiming the sum of £120 for a replacement suit and £10
paid to the dry cleaners (Mr Scrub, receipt enclosed) making
a total of £130.

If I do not receive a cheque for this amount within 14 days
then I will pursue the matter through my solicitor.

Yours sincerely,

Fig. 1.   Sample complaint letter.

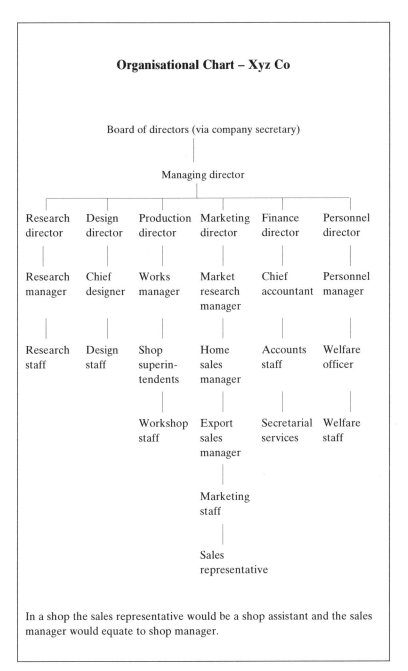

Organisational Chart – Xyz Co

Board of directors (via company secretary)

Managing director

Research director	Design director	Production director	Marketing director	Finance director	Personnel director
Research manager	Chief designer	Works manager	Market research manager	Chief accountant	Personnel manager
Research staff	Design staff	Shop superintendents	Home sales manager	Accounts staff	Welfare officer
		Workshop staff	Export sales manager	Secretarial services	Welfare staff
			Marketing staff		
			Sales representative		

In a shop the sales representative would be a shop assistant and the sales manager would equate to shop manager.

Fig. 2.   Organisational structure of large firms.

- Send a copy letter to their superior, stating that no response has been received.

See Figure 2 for the organisational structure of large firms.

WHEN GROUP ACTION IS APPROPRIATE

So far the emphasis has been on you as an individual, yet if your intended goal would help others then it is not unfair to ask their support. This will relate to matters such as a school closing, roads being re-routed, building of supermarkets and so on.

What to consider when thinking of group actions

Advantages

- Many voices are more likely to be listened to than just one.

- Chance of individual skills being made available at no cost.

- Less easily demoralised by setbacks.

- Mutual support and assistance make you more resilient.

Disadvantages

- You may have had enough but carry on to save face.

- You may be outvoted on what you see as fair results.

- Loss of overall control.

Canvassing initial support

How do you find out if there is any support for your cause? This is usually discovered by talking with friends, work colleagues and so on. It may be worth putting a letter into the local press and asking for like-minded public to contact you directly. When contacted note their name, address, phone number and skills they could bring to the group, type their details out and prepare for the first meeting. Many of the topics already covered in this chapter will apply to a group as well as individuals, even though the scale of the complaint is larger.

Guidelines for organisers

To act as a group everyone should have an opportunity to express their views and these may sometimes be conflicting. It is best to organise a committee with appropriately skilled persons doing certain tasks. Someone who can type can be secretary, a printer can do the pamphlets and so on. It is essential to elect a chairperson and treasurer.

Holding a meeting

This may seem daunting at first but intially should be viewed as a get-together with friends. Try to find out when they are generally available. Preparing a statement of exactly what the group is trying to achieve may sound a bit obvious but will help to keep matters focused.

Hand out the prepared sheets with names and so on. This introduces everybody and means that they can confer with each other to become one effective unit. Some basic points you need to remember:

- The venue should be quiet, light and have refreshments located nearby.

- Highlight the different skills within the group and if possible form a committee.

- Try to stick to an agenda until all points have been covered, then allow time for informal chatting.

- Invite along any other persons you feel may benefit your cause such as councillors, journalists etc.

- Try to obtain a local celebrity or MP to address the meeting with a brief speech. This helps attract media attention.

Why do we need a chairperson?

A chairperson will generally oversee that the agenda is covered and try to keep the group on track. It is very easy for a group of like-minded individuals to pair off and chat about other matters and therefore resolve nothing.

Why do we need a treasurer?

Without financial control a divide will soon open up within the group. One person may not mind buying a few stamps to start with, but if prolonged may feel the financial burden is unfair, especially if the majority of the group do not contribute. Most of the group will give their time for free, but if a fair sum is set aside for each member to cover the cost of stamps, photocopying and so on then it is fair on everyone. The main duties of the treasurer should be:

- Prepare an estaimate of the campaign on a monthly basis.

- Work out how much each member should contribute.

- Collect all monies and allocate funds as needed.

- Keep a record of money coming in and handed out.

What type of action?
The type of action required to resolve a dispute will vary greatly and depend on the opponent. If your action is against someone in the public eye, such as a local politician, then seeking local newspaper assistance would probably be quite effective. A national company would best be targeted via national newspapers and so on. The most obvious type of action is a petition, although these are mainly ignored unless there are many signatories and it is handed to a prominent person in a blaze of publicity.

Demonstrations
As far as the law is concerned you do not need permission to demonstrate, but a local bye-law may exist so check with the town hall. The police can, however, regulate your route if they fear it may provoke disorder. You must give the police 48 hours' notice if you intend to use a loudspeaker. If the demonstration is on private property the owner can use 'reasonable force' to eject the trespassers and possibly sue. To gain maximum benefit from a demonstration:

- Invite all the media you can muster.

- Make sure placards and banners are visible from a distance and instantly understandable.

- Distribute leaflets along the route.

- Consider a photogenic, eye-catching gimmick which shows your point and that you are reasonable people.

- Ask a well-known person to lead.

CASE STUDY

John is happy with his fries

John purchases a meal from a leading fast food restaurant. After finishing his meal he notices a beetle crawling out of the empty packaging. He thinks for a moment and decides to mention the beetle to the store manager in the hope of some free fries. The manager thanks John and gladly gives him a free portion of fries and says the beetle will be disposed of. John leaves the restaurant with his fries feeling that he has done well by mentioning the matter.

In this study John was successful because he:

- Knew when to complain – straight away.

- Defined his goals – he was after a free portion of fries.

- Got to the right person – the manager could rectify, not the counter assistant.

- Supported his claim – had the beetle as evidence.

DISCUSSION POINTS

1. Should John have asked for more in the way of compensation? What would you have asked for?

2. Did he do the right thing in letting the manager dispose of the beetle or should he have taken it to the environmental health department?

3. By letting the manager dispose of the beetle has he foregone any future path of action?

CHECKLIST

1. Is your action taken maliciously or do you have a point to make?

2. Make sure you draw attention to the problem in a reasonable time.

3. Define your goals to ensure they are worth the time and inconvenience of complaining at all.

2

Personal Injury

Nobody wants to have accidents and the greatest hurdle to cover is the initial disorientation. Matters which are important at the time will take precedence and you may well say something which you will later regret. If you are incapable of physically obtaining evidence, whether it be photos, names of witnesses or whatever, then delegate someone else to do it for you. If you can get the other party to admit liability in front of a witness then great, but do not admit any fault on your part as this will count badly against you. If you are attending the scene of an accident and are not a trained first aider, the ambulance service can give you first aid commands over the phone until help arrives.

To pursue a successful claim for damages the other party must have made a fault against you. This comes under the law of tort, a medieval word meaning fault. Everybody owes a duty of care to others. If you can prove that this duty was broken and this caused injury or loss then a claim can be made.

FIRST STEPS IN MAKING A CLAIM

The first action is to decide whether to involve the emergency services. This will obviously depend on the severity of the accident. If you suspect that you have damaged yourself badly then it is always wise to call an ambulance. Your initial thoughts should concentrate on staying calm and collating details which will be needed later. We are not used to a mass of attention so the calmer you are the more easily you can think and describe symptoms to medics which will help them treat you more effectively.

I recommend however that you carry a data card. Leave it in your purse or wallet in case you are not conscious at the time. On your data card you should have:

- blood group

- lists of any allergies

- your own doctor's details

- contact address for next of kin

- your name and address.

If you are treated in hospital
Try to obtain as many details, written down if possible, before leaving the incident site or get somebody who knows the details to come with you to hospital. They can then note their own details and a statement of events which will help later.

When you are treated try to remember who treated you so that they may be traced later if required. Arrange to see a solicitor and your own GP as soon as possible after the event.

PHOTOGRAPHIC EVIDENCE

Photographic evidence is invaluable in many cases as it captures the severity of injuries perfectly. It is especially helpful when the injury is a short-term problem such as a cut, graze, burn or bruise. An indication of date is also extremely useful. The easiest way of confirming this is to include the newspaper of the day as part of the photograph itself.

It is essential to give an indication of scale of an injury site. Any object will do as long as it can be produced later but a coin, ruler, credit card or even a tin of beans is ideal as they can be easily visualised or reproduced. Many parts of the body are impossible to self-photograph easily so enlist help. If the body area which needs to be photographed is in a location you would prefer to keep to yourself you have various options:

- Ask someone to keep guard whilst you use a photo booth.

- Ask the hospital staff to photograph the site for you.

- Purchase a camera with a timer facility and try to obtain a photograph whilst being a contortionist.

If the photographs could possibly offend then you must let the photographic developers know in advance that the prints will be of a sensitive nature. If you feel that this would cause embarrassment then you can always hand the film to your solicitor who will arrange development for you.

How many photos are needed will depend on the location of the accident site. A supermarket fall would require only one or two whereas a large motor accident will require many.

When taking photos the following points should be observed:

- Take them as soon as possible.

- For a motor accident take close-ups of vehicle damage and layouts before the vehicles have been moved.

- If outside take long-distance shots showing site surroundings and road layout.

A picture paints a thousand words and a photograph can show a solicitor details you may have overlooked, to aid your claim. These may range from an overgrown road warning sign, to skid marks indicating speeding, to a local schoolyard where children would have been playing at the time of the accident.

KEEPING A DIARY OF EVENTS

A diary is an excellent reference for any claim as it lists vital information. It has a full day-by-day report of a person's symptoms and can help your GP and solicitor enormously. The best method of record-keeping is to buy a new diary for each claim. It should be large enough to have room for long entries. An ideal size would be an A5 day-a-page diary. Backtrack recent events to the morning of the accident and start filling in.

Details noted should include:

- name and address

- your own doctor's details

- solicitor's details

- medication prescribed, including dosage

- level of pain on daily basis

- appointments

- name and station of attending medical staff
- name and rank of attending police.

SEEKING MEDICAL DOCUMENTATION

Medical evidence is going to be a vital part of any claim for damages. Without it no solicitor can act and no legal action be taken. The more evidence you can supply the better. It is no good going to see a doctor about a fall after the injury has healed.

Tell the doctor and hospital staff that you will be making a claim. They can then tailor their reports in a format suitable for handing to a solicitor at a later date.

If treated as an in-patient you may well be passed around a fair bit. If you cannot remember what treatment you received whilst in hospital then contact the nurse in charge who should compile the information on your behalf.

The nurse in charge will also help you:

- Claim any social security benefits whilst in hospital.
- Arrange social service help if appropriate.
- Arrange a suitable time for a solicitor to visit.
- Organise a discharge notice.
- Refer your file on to the appropriate department for further treatment to be given.

Ensure that you keep all appointments for whichever medical treatment facility you are referred to. If you are on a tight income then the Benefits Agency will provide a refund for travel costs to and from hospital appointments.

WHEN TO INVOLVE THE POLICE

The police should be called to any accident which has caused bodily injury and is the result of someone breaking the law. Many laws are in place to protect the general public against the minority who disregard them.

Contrary to general belief, if the police ask someone to assist in their enquiries or accompany them to the station the accused can actually refuse. The only option is then to arrest them. Only in works of fiction is a suspect 'taken into custody for questioning'; in reality the police have never had this power.

If you suspect that a law has been broken then always inform the police. Remember they can be invaluable as witnesses to collaborate that there was a breach of duty of care towards you. Their presence will add great weight to your claim; the other party may have disregarded you but if you state you can produce a police statement to confirm events they may be more compliant.

As well as assisting with your own claim the police can obviously take action in their own right. Some events come under criminal as well as civil laws. Examples are:

- assault

- injury by an animal

- injury on a building site

- injury at work

- injury whilst visiting another household (see below).

COMPENSATION FROM INSURANCE POLICIES

Although the main claim you have will be against the person or persons whose fault you believe it was, there are other sources of compensation open to you:

- household insurance policy

- personal accident insurance

- employer's medical insurance

- travel insurance.

Household insurance policies

Any personal injury claim made whilst on private property will be made against the occupier of the property. Such a claim, although made against the occupier, would actually be covered by their household insurance policy.

All household policies have a section covering the general public for claims up to one million pounds. There are, however, some clauses which will nullify the claim and so a private claim against the owner would need to be made.

These exclusions will normally include:

- If the injured person is a member of domestic staff.

- Injuries were incurred whilst on the premises to conduct business.

- Caused by mechanically propelled machinery such as lifts, motorhomes, hovercraft, watercraft but not motorised garden equipment.

- Injuries were caused by a dog listed as dangerous by the Dangerous Dogs Act 1991.

There are different liabilities relating to tenants and domestic employees and separate insurance should be taken out if appropriate.

Personal accident insurance

As the name implies this is insurance taken out by yourself to award you compensation because of an accident. Such insurance payouts are not reduced by any other payments you are awarded from other parties. As long as you have fulfilled your obligation to the insurance company involved then a claim can be made straight away, even if the problem may be long-lasting. One of the major benefits of this type of insurance is that you do not have to prove negligence in order to receive it.

There are however some exclusions to policies of this type:

- Injured whilst undertaking a hazardous activity.

- Injured whilst exposing oneself to danger unnecessarily.

- Injured whilst influenced by drink or unprescribed drugs.

- Disablement or injury due to pre-existing health problems.

- Some insurance companies will not cover at all until the policy has been running for a set time.

You should inform the insurers as soon as possible so that a claim form can be sent. There will usually be a set period (normally one to two years) within which the claim must be made.

Typical levels of cover

The amount paid will depend on what level of insurance you have purchased. There is a significant difference between insurance companies in this area but cover is normally resonably priced.

The following figures are from the author's own policy which costs £10 per month.

- permanent total disability (£60,000)

- loss of sight (£30,000 per eye)

- loss of use of limb (£30,000 each)

- loss of speech (£30,000)

- total loss of hearing (£30,000)

- quadriplegia, paraplegia or brain damage (£60,000)

- death (£30,000)

- hospitalisation (£60 per day).

Employer's medical insurance

Again fairly self-explanatory: the employer pays into a scheme on the employee's behalf in case the latter becomes incapacitated and cannot work. They cannot however insure themselves against any claims based on the fact that they did not comply with current health and safety rules. Some policies are double-edged as they cover the employer as well as the employee.

Travel insurance

Many tour operators now have the facility to issue travel insurance via a form printed in brochures. You do not have to take up this insurance and you may be able to get an equally good policy via your own household insurance company. More details on this type of insurance can be found in Chapter 9.

CLAIMING FROM THE STATE

Criminal Injuries Compensation Scheme

The Criminal Injuries Compensation Authority (CICA) was formed to compensate persons who are injured as the result of a crime or suspected crime. There are many areas of physical or mental injury covered in the scheme's list of claimable injuries so there is nothing to lose in making a claim. The authority will also consider loss of earnings and future earnings if disability lasts over 28 weeks.

One of the main benefits of this scheme is that you do not need to have legal assistance in order for a claim to be made.

The main rules relating to the board are:

- Police must be called with minimum delay, whether they can be of assistance or not.

- All claims must be made within two years.

- Reduction in award if victim has 'dubious character'.

- The board has full access to police, employer and medical records.

- If award is given and then compensation is awarded from another source then under certain circumstances the CICA can claim a refund of their award.

- Injury must have occurred in Great Britain, or near the coast whilst on a British registered and controlled aircraft, hovercraft, boat or ship.

- Claimant must assist police, if appropriate, to secure a conviction against the assailant.

What you can claim for
The authority will consider a crime of violence as being the result of:

- any physical or mental injury, although not stress alone

- attempting to stop, or stopping, a criminal

- a fight in which you were an innocent party or bystander

- if you were poisoned

- if you were injured as a result of arson

- injuries caused by a dog being set on you

- deliberately injured with use of a motor vehicle.

Deciding who should claim
In most cases only the victim can claim. There are however some exceptions where this would be impossible or improper. The three exceptions are:

- Relatives or dependants of a victim who has since died.

- A person who is properly authorised to act for an adult who is legally incapable of managing their own affairs.

- The parent, guardian or legal representative of a victim under 18 years of age.

Family violence and/or sexual abuse
The authority will consider applications for such acts and disregard whether the victim was part of the same family as the assailant. However, the rules relating to such claims are more restrictive because of the temptation of fraud. The board will entertain an application if:

- The offender was prosecuted (whether convicted or not).

- The offender will not benefit from the award.

Compensation levels
In theory the board aims to award a similar sum to that which would be awarded via a claim in the civil courts. In practice they are slightly more lean. Hardship caused by lost earnings (less money received from the state) will be considered if appropraite. Each type of injury has been assigned a level of compensation.

Some typical levels of compensation would be:

- sprained ankle (lasting 6-13 weeks) – level 1 – £1,000

- minor head burn – level 3 – £1,500

- dislocated jaw – level 5 – £2,000

- detached retina – level 10 – £5,000

- loss of sight in one eye – level 17 – £20,000

- serious permanent brain damage – level 25 – £250,000.

These figures are only a guide as each injury is individually assessed. If there are multiple injuries then the award given is not a total of the separate areas added together. In this case the main injury would be paid in full, the second injury valued at 10 per cent and the third worst injury at 5 per cent.

The Benefits Agency

Various allowances are claimable through the welfare state. These range from short-term assistance with loss of income to long-term disablement benefit. The main areas to consider are:

- Statutory Sick Pay
- Disability Living Allowance
- Reduced Earnings Allowance.

More information is available from your local benefits agency or via their internet address (http://www.dss.gov.uk/ba) or email site (baadmin@baadmin.demon.co.uk). They have information leaflets in Braille, large type or audio cassette for almost all languages. Their postal address and telephone number is in the phone book under Benefits Agency.

CASE STUDY

John needs a drink

Fresh from his success at obtaining his free portion of fries, John decides to treat himself to a bottle of wine. Whilst reading the label he trips over a badly-laid, loose kerb edging, and takes most of the impact with his right knee and hand. The next morning John cannot move his knee without severe pain. He visits the doctor who classes his injury as a bruised tendon and prescribes two days' rest.

John decides to claim the two days' lost wages from the council and writes to them explaining what happened. The council has already repaired the offending edging and refuses to compensate John. They argue that the edging wasn't that bad and he should have been looking where he was going and not reading a label.

In this case John was not successful because he:

- Did not obtain photographic evidence of the edging.
- Has lost two days' wages.

- Was genuinely not watching where he was going.
- Did not ask for compensation for his injuries.

DISCUSSION POINTS

1. Is it fair for the council to deny John compensation because of his inattention to his path ahead?

2. Would the council have been more generous to John if he had photographic evidence of the state of the edging and intended to seek legal help if not compensated?

3. Would the council have been more generous to John if he was put on prescribed medication as opposed to resting his knee?

3

Motoring

There are many rules and regulations relating to roads and motoring in general. Twenty-one basic laws alone are listed in the rear of the Highway Code.

On average ten people a day are killed in road accidents. When a driver is convicted of breaking the law they will be punished by points being placed on their licence, removal of licence, fine or even imprisonment. All of these punishments are via criminal law but you are obviously open to sue for civil damages if appropriate.

If you are involved in an accident which damages vehicles, animals (except cats), property or persons you must stop as soon as possible and give the following details to the relevant parties:

- your name and address

- vehicle owner's name and address

- vehicle registration number

- insurance details.

As soon as possible after an accident you should report it to the police, certainly within 24 hours. If you do not have your insurance details available at the time of the accident you will have seven days to produce them at a police station.

PENALTIES

Experienced drivers
The penalty point system exists to deter unsafe driving. After being convicted of an offence the driving licence is sent to Swansea where the DVLC will print on the points. The amount of points levied onto the licence is set by government, the most serious crimes obviously receiving the most points (see Figure 3).

If a driver exceeds 12 points in a three-year time span they will be disqualified for a minimum of 6 months.

Offence	Prison	Fine	Disqualified	Points
Causing death by dangerous driving	10 years	unlimited	2 years+	3-11
Dangerous driving	2 years	unlimited	obligatory	3-11
Causing death whilst under influence of drink or drugs	10 years	unlimited	2 years+	3-11
Careless driving	–	£2,500	discretionary	3-9
Driving whilst under the influence of drink or drugs	6 months	£5,000	obligatory	3-11
Failing to stop after or report an accident	6 months	£5,000	discretionary	5-10
Driving when disqualified	6-12 months	£5,000	discretionary	6
Driving whilst having no licence on medical grounds	6 months	£5,000	discretionary	3-6
Driving without insurance	–	£5,000	discretionary	6-8
Speeding – general roads	–	£1,000	discretionary	3-6
Speeding – motorways	–	£2,500	discretionary	3-6
Traffic light offences	–	£1,000	discretionary	3
No MOT certificate	–	£1,000	–	–
Failure to identify driver of a vehicle	–	£1,000	discretionary	3

Fig. 3.   Motoring penalties.

The courts have discretionary powers to remove a licence for any point-incurring driving offence to give the driver time to consider their actions. This is usually for a short time, usually around two weeks. In serious cases the court can even order the driver to re-take a driving test.

New drivers
The rules for new drivers, meaning drivers who have held a full licence for under two years, are slightly different from those for the above. If their licence receives six points then it is revoked and they have to take their test all over again to get it back. If they pass then the two-year limit begins again. This rule, however, only affects the type of vehicle on which the person actually committed the offence.

THE DRIVING LICENCE

The DVLA has recently brought out a new type of photocard licence in a measure to combat fraud. The new type of plastic card licence is available from the DVLA. The card includes a photograph of the driver and a copy of their signature. There is also a separate paper section which will contain details of any endorsements and provisional entitlements. Drivers with the old type of paper licence can change to a photocard licence for a small charge, details are available from your nearest main post office.

Any person over 16 can apply for a provisional driving licence but it will only be valid from your 17th birthday. All applicants must disclose details of any problem which could or would affect their driving.

Some examples would include:

- Epileptic events (seizures or fits).

- Sudden attacks of giddiness, confusion, fainting or blackouts.

- Heart problems (pacemaker, bypass, angina, anti-ventricular tachycardia device).

- Diabetes.

- Parkinson's disease.

- Mental handicap, disorder, memory problems or neurological condition.

- Brain surgery or tumour treatment.

- Stroke.

- Eyesight problems which affect both eyes, but not long/ short-sightedness or colour blindness.

- Major head injury requiring stay in hospital.

- Any difficulties in use of arms or legs.

It is a criminal offence not to disclose any of the above. Your eyesight should be of a standard to read a normal sized number plate from 67 feet (20.5 metres).

If a driver becomes unfit to drive through a disability or accident the DVLC must legally be informed. They may ask you to attend a medical to prove you are fit to drive.

MAIN DRIVER FAULTS

The majority of driver faults revolve around:

- lack of concentration

- seat belts

- speeding.

Lack of concentration

Recent inventions in driver and communication aids are a great boon to the driver but can be distracting if used incorrectly. Whilst travelling the use of many of these aids or modifications by the driver is illegal. Remember that it is illegal to drive without being in full control of the vehicle at all times.

Common distractions which may be deemed to contribute towards loss of control are:

- loud music (cannot hear emergency sirens)

- trying to read maps

- inserting a CD, cassette or tuning a radio

- arguing with passengers or other road users

- eating and drinking.

It is illegal for the driver to use a mobile phone, even a vehicle installed variety, whilst in charge of a motor vehicle. If you are involved in an accident whilst using a mobile your insurance company will still pay the other party for personal injury and possibly property damage, but will then claim the full cost plus their expenses back from you.

Some aids are safe to use whilst driving as long as they do not distract your attention. Indeed some are designed to be used whilst driving. Such items as navigation systems and traffic congestion information systems are perfectly safe and legal.

Seat belts

Wearing a seat belt in the front seat of a car has been a legal requirement since 1983 and then amended in 1993. The law does not prevent you from carrying more passengers than there are restraints but available restraints must be used if available. It is now the driver's legal responsibility to ensure that they not only wear a belt themselves but that the rules below are followed.

Children under 1 year

- Front seat: not allowed, even if held by an adult.

- Rear seat: appropriate child seat must be used.

Children under 3 years

- Front seat: appropriate child restraint must be used.

- Rear seat: appropriate child seat must be used if available.

Child aged 3 to 11 (and under 1.5m tall)

- Front seat: appropriate child seat must be used if available, if not then adult belt may be worn.

- Rear seat: appropriate child seat must be used if available, if not then adult belt may be worn.

Children 12 or 13 (or over 1.5m tall)

- Front seat: adult belt may be worn if available.

- Rear seat: adult belt may be worn if available.

Adult passengers
The same rules apply for adults as for children aged 12 and over but it is their own responsibility, not the driver's to actually wear them. If caught the driver will liable for a fine of up to £1,000.

Exempt vehicles
The rules are not comprehensive and under certain circumstances they do not apply.
   Such vehicles and situations would include:

- Rear seats of cars and small minibuses with an unladen weight of over 2540 kilos.

- Vehicles designed specifically for deliveries.

- Driver who is performing a manoeuvre which includes reversing.

- Delivery vehicles on rounds.

- Licensed hackney carriage drivers.

- Private hire vehicles carrying fare-paying passengers.

- Vehicles used by emergency servies.

- Registered examiners conducting driving test.

Exceptional circumstances
Sometimes the law relating to seat belts does not apply. If a driver feels that for some reason they cannot wear a belt then their doctor can issue an exempt notice.

Speeding
Obviously dangerous but easily done, speeding contributes to many road accidents. One of the main problem areas is when slowing from motorway speeds into town centres where it is especially difficult to gauge the speed you are travelling at. Remember the speed limit is exacatly that, a limit. It is not a target to aim at and should always be treated as a maximum safe speed in perfect conditions (see Figure 4). Lower speed limits are levied on certain vehicles such as caravans and towed trailers. It is illegal to travel in either a caravan or towed trailer.
   Many sections of road now have cameras to record your speed and almost all sections of motorways have camera surveillance.

Type of vehicle	Built-up areas	Carriageways single	double	Motor-ways
Car and motorcycle	30	60	70	70
Car towing caravan or trailer	30	50	60	60
Bus or coach (under 12 metres long)	30	50	60	70
Goods vehicles (under 7.5 tonnes maximum laden weight)	30	50	60	70
Goods vehicles with trailer (under 7.5 tonnes maximum laden weight)	30	50	60	60
Goods vehicles (over 7.5 tonnes maximum laden weight)	30	40	50	60

Stopping distances – feet (metres)

Speed	Thinking	Braking	Total
20 mph	20 (6)	20 (6)	40 (12)
30 mph	30 (9)	45 (14)	75 (23)
40 mph	40 (12)	80 (24)	120 (36)
50 mph	50 (15)	125 (38)	175 (53)
60 mph	60 (18)	180 (55)	240 (73)
70 mph	70 (21)	245 (75)	315 (96)

Fig. 4. Speed limits and braking distances. (Speed shown in MPH.)

The majority of 'A' roads were de-trunked in April 2000 and handed back to local councils. These roads are expensive to repair and speed cameras provide welcome income for their roads programme so expect to see more around.

The court can impose various penalties according to the severity of the offence. In a built-up area the fine could be up to £1,000, if on the motorway this could rise to £2,500. They may also decide to affix penalty points or even disqualify the driver completely. If the offence led to a death then the court could sentence the driver to up to ten years in jail, an unlimited fine and instant disqualification.

ESSENTIAL DOCUMENTS

Almost all road vehicles must have four documents in order to be driven legally on the road. These documents should be kept together in a safe place.

These are:

- Ministry of Transport (MOT) certificate

- tax disc

- insurance

- registration document.

Ministry of Transport (MOT) certificate

If a driver has an accident and the vehicle did not have such a document then insurance may well be invalidated. The only exceptions to this rule are:

- When the vehicle is being driven to an MOT testing station where it has been booked in for a test. In this situation the driver is covered as long as they are on a reasonably direct route to or from the test station.

- If the car was registered as new within three years.

The MOT test covers many areas but is primarily concerned with ensuring the car is safe to drive on the public highway. The areas to be tested on a vehicle are laid down by government, and examiners have to be qualified by the Department of Transport.

Failure to produce a current certificate if requested by police will result in a fine of up to £1,000.

The areas covered on every test include:

- tyres

- brakes

- overall condition (dangerous bodywork etc)

- steering

- horn

- lights.

If the driver knows of any fault that occurs to the car between MOTs, such as a broken light, and then continues to use the vehicle regardless, insurance may be nullified if involved in an accident. The police can also stop any vehicle for a spot-check and instruct the driver to rectify certain faults within a set time then drive the car to the police station for inspection by an officer to confirm rectification of the fault.

Road Fund Licence

This is otherwise known as the tax disc and is a charge levied by the government for using the road. Current legislation now favours owners of smaller engined cars by reducing this liability. Different rates of charge are levied on different types of vehicle and these often change every budget year. Current details are displayed in your general post office.

Some older vehicles are exempt from this charge. If your vehicle no longer needs a tax disc you may claim a refund for the time it is no longer required. The amount of refund (in full months only) will obviously depend on how much the disc cost and the number of months it was used for. If you wish to claim a refund then the disc must be returned, along with the appropriate form (V14) available from the post office. Your local post office or the DVLA will have current details.

Insurance

Contrary to normal belief not every vehicle which uses the road has to have individual insurance; sometimes a fleet company or large business may be self-insured. In effect this means that they have shown that they have sufficient financial resources set aside to meet all claims that could be made against them.

Even if the vehicle is placed upon bricks, as long as it is based on the road it must be insured. Various levels of insurance are available and covered in the next section.

Vehicle registration document (V5)

This is affectionately known as the log book and indeed used to be in the form of a small booklet. Modern vehicle registration documents serve to confirm who actually owns the vehicle. Other details include:

- make and model of vehicle

- date of registration

- registration (number plate)

- chassis number

- engine number.

The document consists of two sections. It is separated and sent off to the DVLA in Swansea when the vehicle is sold or scrapped.

IF YOU SUSPECT DRINK OR DRUGS

If you suspect that the other party involved in a driving accident was unfit to drive through drink or drugs then call the police immediately.

A police officer will carry out tests and if the driver fails them it also becomes a criminal matter. Sometimes the driver may have a special reason for being drunk, spiked drinks being the most common, but the police and courts are used to such excuses and they do not usually accept them.

If you suspect that another driver has used drugs or had a drink you must call the police immediately.

If you think the police have not handled the matter correctly, or you have any matters you may wish to refer to a more senior officer, write directly to the next officer up the chain of command (see Figure 5).

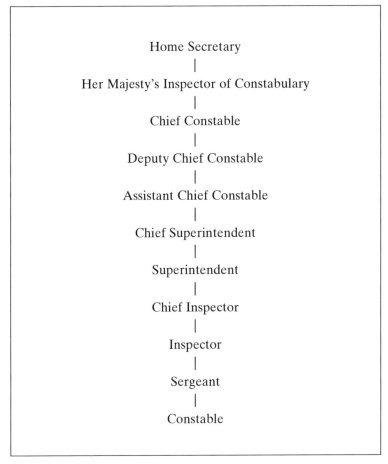

Home Secretary
|
Her Majesty's Inspector of Constabulary
|
Chief Constable
|
Deputy Chief Constable
|
Assistant Chief Constable
|
Chief Superintendent
|
Superintendent
|
Chief Inspector
|
Inspector
|
Sergeant
|
Constable

Fig. 5. Structure of the British police force.

WAS THE OTHER VEHICLE ROADWORTHY?

If you suspect that the other vehicle was in an unroadworthy condition at the time of the accident there are certain areas you should look into. If you can prove that the other vehicle was not fit for public road use the other driver will have no defence against any claim on your part. If the accident was so severe as to warrant recovery of the vehicle to an accident centre your insurance company's loss adjuster will thoroughly check the car.

If you suspect your own car is now unroadworthy because of the accident you should call your own insurance company who will arrange collection of your vehicle. You must inform your insurance company of any accidents, even those which will not generate a claim against you.

After a minor accident you should examine any undamaged areas on the other vehicle to check that it was in a roadworthy condition prior to the accident. If you discover any areas that you consider may have made the car illegal to drive then inform the police immediately and take a photograph of it as well as those suggested in Chapter 2.

Tyres
Tyres can get worn out between MOT tests. The main area where front tyres are prone to wear is on the inside edges, due to incorrect tracking. The law relating to the state of tyres is that:

- The depth of tread is at least 1.6mm.

- The tread must cover the entire circumference of the tyre.

- The tread must cover the central three-quarters of the breadth of the tyre.

- The tyre should be of the correct pressure.

Windscreen, lights, indicators and number plates
All of these areas must be reasonably clean and free from defect.

It is almost impossible to physically check every single area which would be covered in an MOT after an accident. This is where the police can intervene, they can arrange for the car to be collected.

MOTOR INSURANCE EXPLAINED

The majority of vehicles on the road have private insurance, arranged directly with the company or via a broker. Some insurance companies are tailored to a specific type of driver or vehicle. Premiums (the money you have to pay) can vary enormously between companies. If your vehicle is unusual it may be a good idea to join a club for that particular type. Most insurance companies have top-ups to insurance schemes, such as legal cover, which can be very useful.

No-claims bonus (NCB)

As a reward to drivers who do not have accidents the insurance company will issue you with a no-claims discount. The level of discount will depend on how long you have been driving and can be passed between insurance companies. Although you must inform your insurance company of accidents, you do not always have to claim. Occasionally a small accident such as running over a parked bicycle whilst reversing may be much more cost effectively handled directly. A new bicycle may be £200 but if a claim is made your NCB may be lost and this may cost you much more. Remember also that you will lose successive discounts as the years roll by.

Excess

This varies greatly but is essentially a deterrent against small claims being made against the policy. The excess is the initial portion of a claim for which the insurance company will not be held liable.

Principal forms of insurance

There are three principal forms of insurance. Each has certain additional benefits over the last and of course increases in price.

Third party only cover
Many people do not know who the third party is: as far as insurance is concerned you are the first party, your insurance company is the second party and the person you have had the accident with is the third party. As the name implies this level of insurance will pay out to the other person only. This is the most basic insurance and should be taken out even if your vehicle is undriveable but on the road.

If you are a passenger in a motor car, or pillion on a motorcycle, you can claim against the other party or even your own driver/ rider if you have been injured through their negligence in reading the road or their standard of driving was erratic or below normal standards. If the law was being broken at the time, however, the insurance company will try to claim any costs back from the rider/driver.

Third party, fire and theft (TPFT)
This is the same as above but with the added cover that if your vehicle catches fire or is stolen then you can claim. However

you must have taken reasonable care to ensure the vehicle was safe.

Fully comprehensive
Getting onto more coverage again, comprehensive insurance will also cover your own claim for damages, even if the accident was your own fault. There may be the facility to protect your no-claims bonus, if you need to claim for repairs for which you were completely fault-free such as vandalism or collision damage to your car whilst it was parked in a car park.

CASE STUDY

John is hit at traffic lights
John is travelling to a late party when he stops in the middle lane of a three-lane junction as instructed to by traffic lights. Cars pull up either side of him and whilst the lights are changing John's car is hit with moderate force from behind. Both adjoining drivers pull over to assist John but he seems fine and refuses their help. The driver and passengers in the other car seem to have been to a good party already and look mildly drunk. The driver's friends are still enjoying very loud music from the car stereo. They exchange insurance details but the other driver's manners, coupled with his friends' taunting, annoys John who gets angry but carries on to his party.

The next morning John calls his insurance company to inform them of the incident. He is told that the other driver is claiming off John, stating John was drunk and did an emergency stop whilst both cars were travelling through the green light and that he has a car full of witnesses who will confirm it was John's fault. Both the driver and his passengers are claiming personal injuries compensation because of constant headaches since the accident.

In this study John again was not successful because he:

• Did not obtain witness details of the other drivers who stopped.

• Has obtained damage to his car.

• Will lose his no-claims bonus.

• Will have to pay his excess from the insurance company.

- Did not call the police (for thinking the other driver was over the limit).

DISCUSSION POINTS

1. Would the other driver have bothered to claim it was John's fault if they knew he had independent witnesses available if needed?

2. Has John got any options open to him other than to hope the insurance company take his word for it? Remember where John was going.

3. Who would have had to pay for the damage caused to John's car if the police had found the other driver was over the limit, the driver or his insurance company?

4

Negligent Repair of Goods

THE LAW RELATING TO REPAIRS

Before considering the laws relating to repairs it is important that the difference between a 'service' and a 'good' is clear. Because of the way the legal system has evolved there is more protection offered to a purchaser of a good than a service.

Defining whether you have actually paid for a good or service may not always be as straightforward as it sounds.

Examples of goods include:

- food
- drink
- cars
- furniture.

Examples of services include:

- dry cleaning
- shoe repairs
- professional fees
- taxi fares.

Examples

After a minor accident your car requires a new door mirror, which is fitted and then falls off a mile from the garage. Although you have physically paid for a mirror (good) your legal ground would be firmly based on the incorrect fitting of the mirror. The fitting was a service.

Your new suit has arrived from the tailor but one arm is shorter than the other. Although you have paid for the tailor to cut, sew etc your legal ground would be based on the finished article, the suit itself was a good.

The Supply of Goods and Services Act 1982

This has obvious similarities with the Sale of Goods Act 1979 but incorporates services. Although the two areas are completely different there is a similar duty of care owed to you under common law.

The Unfair Contract Terms Act

Some dubious repairers try to discourage the public with disclaimers and then rely on such notices when any goods are returned or claims made. By law all disclaimers must pass a 'reasonableness' test. If a claim is made the other party must prove beyond reasonable doubt that they did their best.

Typical examples of disclaimers would include:

- Goods left at owners' risk.

- All breakages must be paid for.

- Cars parked here at owners' risk.

- The management can take no responsibility for loss of items from these lockers.

- No refunds given.

It would be almost impossible for the offending party to prove many of the above were actually fair. Many claims revolve around the other party not taking as much care of goods left in their care as they could have done.

- Event: Left coat with cloakroom staff whilst at a party. Coat had gone when you went to collect.
  – Disclaimer: Goods left at own risk.
  – Law states: They must take care of any coat deposited.

- Event: Child knocks over unstable stack of glasses.
  – Disclaimer: All breakages must be paid for.
  – Law states: They must display goods in a safe manner.

- Event: Sports shirt stolen from locker with faulty lock.
  – Disclaimer: The management can take no responsibility for loss of items from these lockers.
  – Law states: The locker should have had a non-faulty lock.

Trade Descriptions Act

This applies to traders who promise a service to you that they had no intention of honouring and was just a way of getting you to choose their service over a competitor's. This type of breach will generally focus around time.

Typical examples include:

- 24-hour garage
- 1-hour film processing
- same-day delivery
- 4-hour dry cleaning service.

If a service cannot be done in the allotted time because of a genuine problem such as machine failure, evacuation of premises ordered by emergency services and so on then you could not claim. However, if you believe they never had any intention of honouring such a promise then a claim could be made.

PROVING YOU HAVE A CASE

Sometimes goods are not repaired to a correct standard and the repair can fail. To prove you have a case it must be proven beyond all reasonable doubt that the repairer did not do their very best in attempting the repair, with good parts. Occasionally a repairer may state that they will have a go for you but the repair may not work because of the state of the break or other reasons.

Example 1

If the heel on a lady's shoe breaks the repairer may state that the repair may fail because of an unclean break and show this to the customer. If the customer agrees to let him have a try at the repair, and it then fails in the same place, the customer cannot realistically complain to the repairer.

Example 2

Your video recorder develops a fault on the main control board. A repairer fixes the fault only for the same fault to reappear after a few days. The repairer responds with the excuse that the re-placement part must have failed and that he would come out again and repair it for another charge. In this scenario a second fee would not be payable because the repairer used a faulty part. The customer is now free to either let the repairer have another go or get a different company to fix it and the customer would then be free to claim a refund from the original repairer. The latter can reclaim the cost of a replacement part, plus fitting cost from the part manufacturer and hence not be out of pocket.

THE SUPPLY OF GOODS AND SERVICES ACT 1982

All repairers have duties of care to their customers which they must honour.

Duty 1

- Work must be done with reasonable care and skill.

You would not expect an odd-job man to build you a garage to the same standard as a master builder, but you should expect him to do his best.

As is sometimes the case in law the vagueness of the term 'reasonable care and skill' can make it very difficult to prove you were not given this duty.

Most importantly do not pay for work done that does not meet your expectations. It is far easier to deduct from a final bill than to try to get money back. If you suspect that the work is far from their best effort then several remedies are open to you:

- Try to negotiate a lower charge for the service.

- Allow them another go to do it right.

- Seek a second opinion from a tradesperson providing a similar service.

- Seek an opinion from an inspector of a trade body of which they are members.

- Seek an opinion from an expert in the field.

If it can be reasonably shown that the finished job is substandard, and your faith in the original contractor to complete the task no longer exists, you can instruct another company to put it right.

If you have not paid the original invoice
The cost of putting the work right can be deducted from the initial contractor's invoice. In order to get this money from you, that they feel may be owed, they would have to prove the work was to standard and the second contractor was wrong.

As you can appreciate this would be very difficult for them to prove.

If you have paid for the work in full
Before instructing another contractor to begin rectification work, enlist the professional opinion of an expert in the field. The local council, along with Trading Standards, have a wealth of experts in almost every field who would come and inspect on your behalf. If they agree the work could have been much better then you could expect their support if the original contractor disagrees with your opinion.

Notify the original contractor of your intention to get the work done right. It is your choice whether you let them have another try. If you decide the second contractor is your best bet then you need to claim the second contractor's fee back from them. Without a professional opinion backing you this can be quite difficult, as you alone would have to prove they did not do their best.

Sometimes a contractor may ask for part payments of a completed aspect of a job. This is common practice if the task is quite expensive. It is best agreed in writing between yourselves and the contractor before any work starts at all.

This mostly concerns the building trade. For example, if an extension is being built on the side of a house the work may be divided into several parts:

- digging out the foundations
- laying foundations
- bricklaying walls
- fitting roof
- electrical and plumbing
- installation of windows and doors
- fitting ceilings and artex
- plastering and final detailing.

In reality this works well for the builder and customer. The builder gets money in order to fund their costs for the next aspect. It also gives some protection to the building contractor that they will receive some money and not have to shoulder the whole sum if the customer cannot pay upon completion. The customer also benefits because they get to inspect each aspect before payment and can make sure each area is done to their satisfaction before the next.

The council's building regulations department will also often want to inspect each completed task to ensure its own regulations are met.

Duty 2

- Proper materials of suitable quality must be used.

Again this has similarities with the Sale of Goods Act (goods must be fit for purpose). Sometimes it is obviously dangerous to fit parts which are known to be substandard. It is recommended that you use a large, established company when having any repairs done to items which could be life-threatening if they fail.

Examples would include:

- car brakes, suspension, tyres, steering mechanism
- anything electrical
- bicycle brakes.

The reasoning behind this is that larger companies are usually better insured and less likely to simply disappear or change their name slightly and start up again, thereby avoiding any claims made to their previous incarnation. Ideally factory approved parts should be used. Sometimes these are expensive however, and a replacement part which has been tested to British Standards should be fine. If you are injured because of the negligence of the repairer then you can claim for any damage to self or property.

Duty 3

- Goods left in their care should be looked after in a reasonable and responsible manner.

This unfortunately again wanders in legal mist because of the word 'responsible'. If an item is lost by a repairer they will have a difficult task to prove that they took all reasonable steps to ensure the item's protection. Goods that simply disappear are assumed to have been stolen.

In any case the value of the claim will be based on the replacement cost of the lost item. If the item is irreplaceable its value would form the basis of the claim. Sometimes there is an exclusion clause such as 'goods left at your own risk'. This has been covered under the Unfair Contract Terms Act listed earlier.

Duty 4

- The work will be done as agreed.

Occasionally the service provided may not have been the one initially agreed upon by both parties. When this happens the customer is only liable for the work initially agreed upon. For small repairs the work will be obvious, but when larger works are involved it is much more useful to have details put in writing with a maximum figure covered with a phrase such as 'if the job is going to cost more than £50 please contact me before starting.' If the bill then comes to more than £50 and you have not been contacted, the repairer must incur it.

Example
An external decorator has repainted your windows as requested. Upon your return you find that the front door has also been painted. The door was in a poor state of repair anyway and needed painting. The contractor states that he had instructions to paint windows and door and asks for the extra labour charge. You could legally avoid the charge for the door and only pay for the work done on the window frames.

Example
A car is taken for its annual MOT test. The owner explains to the garage that the car is needed for work upon his return from a week away, and instructs the garage to do any work needed and says he will collect the car with its certificate upon return. When the owner returns a large, detailed invoice is looming. The garage explains that the extra work was essential to comply with current Department of Transport rules and followed the instructions given. To make matters worse the garage, feeling that the invoice cannot be paid, insists the account is settled before the car is removed from the premises.

If the owner feels the charge is unreasonably high then he can question the garage, explaining they may have broken the rules regarding 'reasonable price' and ask for a lower labour charge to be levied. If the garage has complied with the four duties owed to the customer they have every right to hold the car until paid and the customer must pay.

WHAT YOU SHOULD EXPECT FROM A FAIR REPAIR

If you have followed the previous advice there should be no means of the repairer avoiding the main duties owed to you.

If the repair does not last very long, and you feel that this implies the work was done with inferior parts or without due care and skill, the item can be returned and a refund obtained. If the failure has caused physical or property injury then they may also be liable. The only exceptions to this are if the repairer feels that:

- The item was not used in its intended way.

- The repair failed after a reasonable time.

- The breakage/fault was not the one previously fixed.

- The failure was down to defective parts which they could not have known were faulty.

That nasty word 'reasonable' has again reared its ugly head and created a mist over the whole issue. The time a repair lasts will depend on the actual item repaired and its usage. To state suitable time limits for each and every type of item would be an unreasonable demand on the court system.

The repairer may get annoyed if you question their standard of workmanship and without a second opinion it can be hard to show this was the case (see Proving You Have a Case on page 54).

If the repairer can show that the work was done with total care and skill, they can claim from you the cost of the work plus any other charges in confirming their claim which will probably include the cost of legal advice.

When a quote cannot be reasonably given
Often a price will be agreed either verbally or via a price list displayed on the repairer's premises.

In some cases a set price would not be appropriate because the contractor cannot define what is wrong, is then unsure of parts needed and the amount of time the job will take. It is then reasonable to let the repairer conduct exploratory work or a survey to ascertain what is wrong and prepare a quote. This is usually given free by the repairer in the hope they will get the go-ahead. Generally this applies to:

- repairs involving large, portable electrical appliances

- car repairs

- plumbing works.

If there is to be a charge for this exploratory work then it should be agreed before any such work is started – their competitor may provide this service for free. If you decide to go ahead without waiting for the results of such work then it is always advisable to set a maximum figure in writing (see example under Duty 4 of Proving you Have a Case on page 58).

If you think your bill is too high
Legally you only have to pay a 'reasonable' price for the work involved. This may depend on how urgent the repair is and even at what hour of the day. It would be reasonable for a 24-hour plumber called out during the night to charge more than for a similar job done in normal working hours. You could obtain a second opinion from a similar firm as to what would have been a reasonable price for the job. There have been many situations where a go-ahead has been given for a repair, without a quote, by unscrupulous tradespersons and the invoice has been very high.
    Never authorise such a job if the tradesperson:

- Is from an unfamiliar company.

- Will not provide a written quotation (even on a scrap of paper).

- Has called without an appointment.

- Will not provide you with identification and give you time to write it down.

- Says that they will want cash.

If any of this happens to you call the police immediately and they will investigate promptly.

Example

A pensioner, living alone, goes to the front door of her house. A man says he has noticed her roof has a few tiles missing which with the bad weather could bring her ceilings down if not fixed straight away. Luckily for the lady he happens to have just enough spare ones in his van parked just around the corner and could pop them up for her without her having to wait for them to come to the area again.

He is polite and cheerful and is given the go-ahead. After the job has been done his workman, a large, rough and mean-looking man, asks her for £500 cash. She becomes frightened and as the work has already been completed she feels she has to pay.

Example

An elderly gentleman is called upon by a pair of workmen dressed in council-type overalls who explain they have been resurfacing a nearby road and have some tarmac left over. They have noticed his drive is looking a bit rough and offer to lay spare tarmac for £20 cash rather than throw it away. The man agrees it would be a waste and gives go ahead, believing he has done well. The man's drive covers about 30 square yards, and at £20 per square yard the bill is £600. He is made to feel that it was his mistake for not understanding them and pays them the £600 after being kindly given a lift to the bank in the lorry.

Your own written quote

These type of rogues typically prey on the meek or old, and are always charming and give the impression they are helping you. If they are genuine they will have no qualms about signing a written quote limiting their bill. Any piece of paper or card will suffice. All that is needed is that you write down the full extent of the job and a maximum figure the work will come to. They should be able to give you a rough idea.

Coming back to the first example the woman could have asked how much, and if told about £25 to £30 then obtained a note stating 'fix broken tiles, work won't cost more than £30'. In the second example a note stating 'lay spare tarmac over drive, total cost £20' would do.

As far as the law is concerned, once they have started the work after signing such a slip, a contract has been formed and they cannot legally ask for more money than previously agreed.

When the repairer can sell your goods

Sometimes goods are abandoned because the owner has decided they do not want them any more. This is particularly true in the shoe repair trade when the owner decides to buy a new pair rather than bother to collect a pair handed in for repair and incur the repairer's bill.

Legally a repairer can sell the goods, deduct any fees owed and then send a payment of the difference left over to the customer. Before they can do this they must contact, or try their best to contact, the customer and inform them of their intent. A time limit should be given for collection, after which the repairer will sell the goods for their current market value. After the goods have been sold there are three possible outcomes:

1. The sale cost did not cover the repairer's costs. The repairer can claim the difference from the customer, via legal action if necessary which obviously increases the bill.

2. The sale cost exactly equalled the repairer's cost. No further action.

3. The sale cost exceeded the repairers costs. The customer could get the difference unless it was agreed in the repairer's contract that no extra money would be recoverable.

If the customer feels that the goods have been sold at too low a price they can take legal action. This would however be pointless if condition 3 above applied. If the repairer feels that the goods may not have legally belonged to the customer they can apply to a local court to approve the sale.

Quotations and estimates

Quotations are binding on both parties, which can work in favour of the customer or contractor depending on the final amount of work needed. If a video repairer thinks only a small part is faulty, and hands a quote of £25 to a customer, then finds it needs a major part, the customer has gained. Likewise the opposite can apply and if on examination only a fuse has blown then the customer would be liable for the £25 charge.

Estimates can be more vague and only give an indication of what the final amount may come to. The figure stated is not binding to either party. If the finished price is way above the estimated price then the contractor has to justify the difference.

If the problem cannot be fixed

If the contractor/repairer has tried their best to resolve the fault but cannot fix it they can charge a reasonable amount for the time taken in their attempt. If the item is then fixed by another repairer the customer can refuse the initial repairer's bill as they should have found the fault. The onus would then fall on them to prove they tried their best. This can be very hard to prove and the claim is normally unpursued.

Late completion of work

If a time limit is important then it must be stated to the repairer, usually with as much warning as possible. Asking for a shoe to be repaired within three days ready for a wedding would be acceptable; calling the TV repair shop and saying you want the set back for tonight's big match would not be. If the work is not done on time then the repairer is liable for a reasonable charge from the customer for any inconvenience caused.

For instance, a man delivers his moped for repair and states it needs to be working in 28 days, the repairer agrees it will be done on time. If after 28 days the moped is still undergoing repairs the man would be allowed to claim:

- hire charge of similar replacement vehicle

- his extra telephone costs chasing the garage

- minimal amount for inconvenience caused.

The garage would have to deduct these charges from the repair cost. If these charges are more than the repair cost then the garage will become liable for the difference.

The man has a legal obligation to the garage, however, to keep his costs to a minimum. Upon receipt of his bill the garage point out that he has an old moped and yet hired a new, large motorcycle. They could deduct the difference between moped and motorcycle hire costs, but not for a new rather than old moped as a hire company would only have new mopeds.

Receipts for repair work.

You are only legally entitled to a receipt for repairs if you are either claiming back the VAT element or preparing a claim under an insurance policy and the receipt is needed. Most repairers will give receipts however, and these should be kept until the good is disposed of as it is proof against them if the repair fails early or the item causes injury.

CASE STUDY

Johns rejects a faulty repair

John's car is taken into the garage to have the repairs carried out from his accident. All seems well, but a few days later whilst on the motorway the replacement bumper falls off and is promptly crushed by a lorry.

John correctly stops where safe and using an emergency phone informs the police of the hazard. Upon his return to the garage the staff say the bumper must have been tampered with by John or damaged by a vandal and hence a new insurance claim, again with payable excess, would be appropriate. John refuses this explanation as he hasn't been out much and knows he did not tamper with anything. He has had enough and informs the garage that he feels it was not fitted properly and will claim a replacement, free of charge, because the repair failed. John has got a good case.

In this case John will succeed because he:

- Did not tamper with the bumper after fitting.

- Has taken responsible care of his car since it was repaired.

- Was travelling on a smooth road which could not have ripped the bumper from its mountings.

DISCUSSION POINTS

1. What laws would relate to this situation?

2. Would his claim be for a 'good' or 'service'?

3. Which government authority should John inform if he feels the garage is trying to cheat him or his insurance company?

5

Shopping

CONSUMER RIGHTS

The golden rule in any purchase for something you are planning to keep for some time is keep the receipt until you dispose of the item. Without this proof of purchase you will find it very difficult to pursue any future claims, whether they involve returning poor quality goods for a refund or taking legal action against the seller should an injury occur.

The main legislation on shopping is the Sale of Goods Act 1979, but in order for any action to be taken a binding contract must be formed. Contracts consist of three main parts:

- offer
- acceptance
- consideration.

Each of these areas is vital in any claim.

Offer
This is when you offer to purchase certain goods. The law has an implied term which covers 'title'. It assumes the item is theirs to sell in the first place and that there are no outstanding finance agreements placed upon the item or items offered for sale.

Acceptance
If the prospect of owning the item has appealed to the customer enough for the purchase to go ahead then the buyer's offer is accepted by the seller.

Consideration
This usually refers to money changing hands, but equally applies to circumstances when a contract is classified as being made. The actual amount of money does not matter.

However, consideration can also mean that the product has

been used and caused some problem, such as a failure in a free sample which causes an injury.

THE CONTRACT

As soon as all three parts of the contract have been formed it becomes binding. Until the final consideration has been handed over either side can refuse to proceed. To quote Sir George Jessel, a nineteenth century judge, 'Contracts when entered into freely and voluntarily shall be held sacred.'

A sample simple contract may consist of the following set of three transactions:

- I'll take the Washing machine in the window for £200 = offer

- Yes sir, how would you like to pay? = acceptance

- Here you are, £200 cash = consideration.

If a customer takes an item which they suspect is priced too low, and the store does not notice until after money has changed hands, then the store cannot request any further money.

Alternatively if the store cashier notices the error of the item being the wrong price before any money has changed hands then the contract may be terminated. If you suspect the store is doing this on purpose then inform your local Trading Standards office as this practice is illegal. As all persons reading this book are the honest type they will obviously seek out an experienced member of staff and confirm the price rather than take the item quickly to an inexperienced till assistant.

The only exceptions to the above rules relate to auction houses and mail order companies. In these circumstances the goods will be considered yours when either the hammer strikes the gavel or the item is posted.

Returning goods

If the customer decided they no longer want the item after completing a contract the seller can claim back the profits lost from the sale. This however would not apply if the goods were returned because they were faulty or did not comply with the main rights given to the consumer under the Act.

Bear in mind that under the Sale of Goods Act only the third rule, relating to the description of goods, applies to private sellers as well as traders. However, if you suspect the individual is actually a trader then consult your local Trading Standards office for advice on whether they would be held liable. It is illegal for traders to claim they are private sellers in an attempt to avoid consumer laws.

Buying direct from an advertisement
If the goods were purchased because of an advertisement seen in a newspaper or magazine then the Mail Order Protection Scheme may help. You should call the publishers to see whether a claim may be made. Be very wary if there is only a post office box number and not a full address. If you are unsure you could ask the local Trading Standards office for advice as to whether they have received many complaints about the company.

Retailers' duties
It may be worth contacting your local Trading Standards by phone to see if they have had any complaints against the sellers. Some goods have manufacturers' guarantees which are useful when your statutory rights no longer apply, but claiming under these guarantees is often a hassle. Some retailers try to pass off their liability by saying that it's the manufacturers fault. Do not be put off by this unless you bought the item some time ago. It is the retailer's problem if goods are faulty and they should sort out the manufacturer directly.

RIGHTS COVERED BY THE SALE OF GOODS ACT 1979

These are sometimes referred to as statutory rights and you may see notices in stores offering additional promises to their customers with the closing line 'this does not affect your statutory rights'. It is illegal for a seller to try to take away these rights or restrict them in any way.

The Act implies three terms, essentially rights to the consumer. That goods are:

- fit for their usual and intended use
- of proper quality
- described correctly.

Each of these areas is explained further below with reference to actual legal cases.

Goods are fit for their usual and intended use

The customer has the right to presume the seller has taken care and skill to select his stock, for instance that a sandwich is fit to eat or a chair is safe to sit on.

Legal case 1

A lady died after drinking milk contaminated with typhoid germs. The decision was in the family's favour as the milk was not fit to drink.

Legal case 2

In Godley v Perry (1960) a 6-year old boy had lost an eye after a cheap (6d) catapult broke after little use. The seller was held liable for selling an unfit product.

Legal case 3

In Wilson v Rickett Cokerall & Co Ltd (1954) a lady who had ordered Coalite fuel was injured when an army detonator was included in the delivery and exploded. She was awarded damages because Coalite mixed with detonators was not fit for burning.

Unusual use

If an item is not used in its usual or intended way this right does not apply. If for instance you broke a shoe when using it to hammer in a nail the seller would not be liable. If a customer states a specific purpose for which the item is intended, and then the item fails, the store would however be liable. If you are not sure whether something you are planning to buy will actually be suitable for the task then confirm with the seller. This will then cover you should the item be unsuitable.

If the seller suspects the item was used in a way it was not intended for then a refund may be refused. There must however be reasonable grounds.

Goods are of proper quality

The actual terminology used in the act refers to goods being of 'merchantable quality'. In this situation the word 'merchantable' is taken as its literal meaning of 'saleable' or 'marketable'.

This creates a grey area in which to apply the law – how do you tell if the goods are of an expected quality? The expectations on sellers would reflect the item's price, the brand name, store's location and so on. You would not expect the same quality of a coat bought for £10 from a budget shop as from a £100 coat bought from a major high street store. Luckily the first right covering 'fit for purpose' overlaps this section and so provides consumer rights.

If upon delivery the item has developed a minor fault and the seller offers to have it repaired then the customer should allow this, even though in theory it could be rejected. The seller could state that the customers is using the minor fault as an excuse to return an item because they have changed their mind and do not want to pay for the seller's lost profits.

Example
A new car is delivered and it is noticed that it has a crack on the side indicator cover. The garage offers to replace the cover free of charge as soon as one is available from the manufacturers. The car will still perform all of the tasks it was designed for so is 'fit for purpose' but the crack makes the finished item of a standard which could be classed as 'unmerchantable'. If however the car kept having various failures then it could be rejected at a later date.

Quality
How long something should last will again depend on the level of quality of the circumstances relating to its sale. The coat from the budget shop would not be expected to last as long as the high street store's wares. If the customer thinks the item should have lasted longer they should return the item and complain.

The only exception to this rule is if a specific fault is pointed out to the customer before the sale is finalised, or the store gives a discount on a specific fault which the customer has pointed out. In either of these two circumstances the goods cannot be returned unless a different fault has been discovered. Sometimes the store may argue that a particular fault should have been spotted by the customer before they bought the item. If the fault is obvious they may refuse a refund. This is a grey area and would depend on each individual situation. It is always wise to inspect goods before you buy them. Obviously this would not apply to goods ordered by mail order which, if found faulty, could be refused and returned.

Legal case 4
In Heil v Hedges (1954) Mr Heil had bought some pork chops from Mr Hedges. When unwrapped the chops were infested with parasitic worms. Mr Heil lost his case because Mr Hedges argued that the chops would have to have been cooked before being eaten and this would have killed the worms.

Goods are described correctly
If an item is sold via a description or statement then the item must comply. Obvious examples would include

- A ham sandwich must contain ham.

- Cotton sheets must contain no nylon.

- Shoes listed as size 9 must be size 9.

- Oxford blue paint must be the right shade.

Legal case 5
In Beale v Taylor (1967) Mr Beale bought a car from Mr Taylor, a Triumph Herald 1200. It later transpired that the car had been made from the front end of one car and the back end of another. As the true engine size was not 1200cc Mr Taylor was sued because the car was 'not as described'.

Descriptions
If a statement is made relating to the item, which is later proved false, then the goods can be returned.

Sometimes however the law becomes nonsensical. Take for example the grand tradition of the market traders and used car salesmen. They have bought phrases to the world of selling that are ingrained into the memories of young and old. Take for example:

- Not £20, not £10, don't even give me £5, who'll give me £3 the lot?

- I'm cutting my own throat here.

- Isn't she a cracker?

- Lovely little runner.

- Pulls the birds.

- Goes like a bomb.

This is pure sales puff, nothing more. If however a specific statement is made either in writing or verbally which is untrue, then the item may be returned and damages sought. Indeed you would not want some of the above to apply – who wants a car that attracts gifts from pigeons and then explodes!

GUARANTEES EXPLAINED

In this context there is really no difference between a guarantee and a warranty. The only main differences appear when contracts are delved into by legal professionals. Both imply a promise from the manufacturer to the consumer that the goods will be of sufficient quality to last for at least the length of time covered by the guarantee.

Most appliances come with some level of guarantee, most with one year from date of purchase. The way in which most manufacturers organise this is to include a guarantee card which the purchaser completes and then posts off. The inclusion of details and postage is actually tantamount to a technical contract with consumer and manufacturer.

Sometimes an extended warranty or guarantee will try to be sold either at the end of the initial guaranteed period or at the time of the initial sale. The shop does very well out of such extended guarantees on a commission basis. Various companies now offer protection against failure and so on for all electrical appliances and may well be cheaper than a policy for each item in the house.

RETURNING FAULTY GOODS

If a fault occurs then the initial step should be with the seller as soon as possible. If they deny responsibility then forward a letter, setting out the complaint in writing. If the item was bought with a credit card then inform the card company as some have insurance cover. Likewise if the goods were bought on credit you may be able to claim against the credit supplier.

It is often very difficult to prove that a product manufacturer has regularly produced faulty goods. To admit to such negligence would leave them undefended against any actions brought against them by Trading Standards and so on.

Goods that are obviously faulty can be returned under the Sale of Goods Act, but it is sometimes difficult to show that a reasonable standard of quality was not achieved. Consumer laws are the cornerstone of claims against traders. They are vital when there is a case for compensation against a manufacturer who produces shoddy goods and whose unsafe product causes injury or loss.

Claiming damages

If the failure of the item has incurred further bills then these should also be claimed back. The onus of the claim then shifts from 'refund' to 'damages'. If, for instance, clothing or other property has been damaged, or time lost off work, then an itemised invoice should be prepared and sent to the seller of the goods in the first place.

Dealing with disputes

If the item is still in the possession of the customer, and the seller disputes the claim, it should not be sent back to the store but held onto in case Trading Standards or an independent engineer need to examine it. You should also extend the option of having the seller carry out their own examination of the item on your premises at their own expense.

RETURNING GOODS WITHOUT A RECEIPT

If you were tricked into signing a contract without being alerted to the various terms expressed in it then the contract is null and void. If a customer signs a contract after checking all the points, sometimes in rather small print, then it is binding. If you were sold goods via a contract which you could show was null and void then a refund would be appropriate.

Example

A suit is cleaned at a local dry cleaners. Upon collection the owner notices it still has many of the marks they had been told would be removed. The manager draws the customer's attention to a small sign on the back of the front door stating they cannot guarantee to remove all marks.

As this notice was placed in an area the customer would have only seen after leaving the garments it could not have formed part of the original contract. If the notice had been on the counter then it would have been in clear view and therefore classed as a valid clause.

Gifts

Sometimes faulty goods are received as gifts. In this case it is the original purchaser who has entered into contract with the shop and technically their responsibility to either exchange or return the item. However, in practice most stores will entertain an exchange with the new owner providing they have the receipt.

WHEN THE STORE CAN AVOID A REFUND

Take for instance a child's coat. After selling a coat a shopkeeper sees the child using it as a sledge to slide down grassy hills. If the coat is returned with rips after a few days the shopkeeper could refuse a refund as the coat was not used as intended.

Many of the larger chain stores have a policy which voluntarily gives extra consumer protection as well as those covered by statutory rights. Most will exchange or give a refund for goods bought in another of their branches provided the item is either exclusive to themselves or has an appropriate receipt.

A store can also refuse to exchange certain items which involve underwear and jewellery. When this is the case a sign is normally visible and the clause mentioned during the initial stages of the sale. This type of exclusion clause is allowed because of health grounds, but if the item is faulty or of poor quality then the normal rules apply and a refund or damages can be sought.

Credit notes

Another remedy which a store can apply is the exchange of goods for a credit note which could be used elsewhere in the same store. However, such a note can be refused if the item did not comply with any of the rights a customer can expect under the Act.

If the item being exchanged is fault-free and the customer has simply changed their mind, then it is reasonable to expect the store to offer a credit note. Study the credit note itself as they sometimes have a validity date.

THE STORE'S ACCIDENT BOOK

Legally all stores must have Public Liability Insurance (PLI) which covers the premises against any legal actions taken against them in the same way as a household policy insures visitors on your premises. The certificate of insurance must be clearly visible to all customers and is usually placed near the entrance. This type of insurance mainly covers injuries to members of the public whilst using the store.

If any injuries are sustained whilst in a store they should be reported to the management who will enter them into a book. If a book is elusive ask for the details to be written down and then signed by the manager. If you then decide to pursue the claim you will have written evidence of the incident. Remember that a small injury can cause problems later so it is always worthwhile getting written proof in case it is needed later.

CASE STUDY

John finds a sole mate

John buys a new pair of shoes and files the receipt. After four weeks the stitching fails and a shoe starts to come apart. He returns the shoes along with the receipt.

The store offers John a partial refund arguing that although the shoes have failed John has had some use of them, for which he is liable. John can see their point and accepts.

In this study John has succeeded because he:

- Did not tamper with the shoes.

- Took responsible care of the shoes.

- Kept the receipt.

DISCUSSION POINTS

1. Was the store being fair in their reduction?

2. Would you advise John to contact Trading Standards?

3. What points could you raise in determining the life span of an item such as a shoe?

6

Animals

ANIMAL LAWS

In all cases involving animals the problem of negligence lies on the claimant's shoulders. In order to claim against the owner of an animal that causes damage to property or personal injury the owner must be shown to have acted negligently. For instance letting a dog off a leash when in the owner's enclosed garden would be fine, but letting it run free in the park would not. Owners of cats whose actions cause injury or damage are however very difficult to claim against as a cat is, by its nature, a wandering animal.

There are however three exemptions to this rule:

- permanently dangerous animals

- occasionally dangerous animals

- livestock.

Permanently dangerous animals

If an owner keeps a dangerous animal then no proof is needed in order to pursue a claim, as the owner knows of the danger beforehand and keeps the animal at their own risk.

To generalise, a dangerous animal is one which is not usually domesticated in this country and would probably cause damage when fully grown. Such animals need permanent supervision. Zoo and circus animals would be included in this category. Any person who has a dangerous wild animal must have a licence, via the local authority. Insurance is sometimes available for damage caused by dangerous animals and should be considered if planning to acquire such an animal.

Occasionally dangerous animals

This covers a normally placid animal who is known by the owner to have occasional bouts when it may be classed as dangerous, albeit temporarily. Again as the owner knew it was a dangerous animal it leaves the owner open to action without the need for proof. This may occur if the animal is expecting a litter or on medication.

Livestock

The owner may be liable whether they were negligent or not. The burden on the claimant is reduced because of this and the owner would have to show they were not negligent in order to avoid a claim. This is normally very difficult for livestock owners to do.

If a rambler opens a field gate and fails to close it properly, allowing cattle to escape and cause damage, the farmer would not be liable as he was not to blame. If the gate was faulty however, the farmer would be liable as they were negligent in not keeping the gate in good order.

Owners of livestock on agricultural land have a law which specifically enables them to shoot and kill and dog which they feel is worrying their livestock or themselves. If livestock are injured or personal injuries sustained then the dog owner can be sued for damages, whether they were actually negligent or not. If a farmer shoots such an animal the incident should be reported to the police as soon as possible (see Cresswell v Sirl [1948] for a legal example).

If livestock have damaged property then the owner of the damaged property can detain the offending livestock for compensation. This only applies if the animal has actually caused damage after straying. In such circumstances the police must be called and the animal given food and water. If the animal itself has become injured the RSPCA should also be called.

Laws relating to the keeping of animals are:

- Dangerous Wild Animals Act 1976

- Animals Act 1971

- Guard Dogs Act 1975

- The Dogs Act 1871 and 1926

- Control of Dogs Order 1930

- Dogs (Protection of Livestock) Act 1953

- Protection of Animals Act 1911

- Abandonment of Animals Act 1960

- Endangered Species (import and export) Act 1976

- The Wildlife and Countryside Act 1981

- Badgers Act 1973

- Conservation of Seals Act 1970

If the owner of the animal is under 16 then the head of the household will be held liable for the damage. Some animals classed as pests can be killed on sight, but not by using snares, explosives or decoys. Such animals would include:

- coypu

- rats

- mice

- foxes.

Importing pets

A 'passport for pets' scheme was introduced in 2000. This enables owners of cats and dogs to travel between European countries as each animal can have blood tests and a digital identification tag inserted by a vet. Scanners at customs points then scan the animal to confirm its history.

The Balai Directive

This is handled by the Ministry of Agriculture and means that a European breeder, with an animal born in their care, can send it direct to a breeder in any other European county. It ensures that the animal has never come into contact with another which could be harbouring disease.

Guard dogs

All guard dogs must be kept either tethered or in the full care of a handler at all times. Only commercial properties which employ the protection of such dogs are covered. All premises using guard dogs must have warning signs indicating this.

RESPONSIBILITIES OF PET OWNERS

All dogs must be registered with the local council. Owners have various responsibilities towards their animals and the general public.

The more common problems include:

- fouling of footpaths
- noise disturbance
- animal mistreatment.

If you suspect that a pet owner is ignoring or has broken such laws then ask your local council for further advice.

Any animal has a legal right not to be treated in a cruel way. It is an offence punishable by a fine, disqualification from future ownership and possible imprisonment.

IF YOU ARE BITTEN BY AN ANIMAL

Germs breed very quickly in an animal's mouth and may be transferred into the wound. Take the following steps quickly.

- Get the owner's details.
- Thoroughly clean the area of the bite with warm water and soap or mild antiseptic.
- If the skin has been broken then dress the wound with a clean cloth or bandage and visit a doctor or outpatients department as soon as possible.
- Report the matter to the police as soon as possible; it will be a great help if you have managed to obtain the identity of the animal's owner.

If you can show that the animal was known to be dangerous to the owner then a civil claim could be made. The old saying 'every dog is allowed one bite' may apply even today, as the owner could say they did not know the dog was dangerous until after the first bite. If you wish to take such action the first step should be in the direction of your own doctor, followed promptly by a visit to your solicitor or your nearest magistrates court.

The prosecutor in such a case would have to show that the dog was not controlled properly and an actual danger, not just a nuisance. If the court decides the dog is indeed dangerous it can impose various punishments on the owner, including the destruction of the animal itself.

WHAT TO DO WITH AN INJURED ANIMAL

In the case of a road accident pull over to the side of the road as soon as possible and try to ascertain if the animal is injured or dead without getting too close as it may attack. Whether the police have to be called will depend on the type of animal. You must report your name, address and vehicle registration number to the police or any other person who has reasonable grounds for requesting them if you kill or injure a:

- horse, ass or mule
- cow or bull
- sheep
- pig
- dog
- goat.

If you injure a wild animal (as opposed to a pet or livestock), and you feel the animal will not recover, then the law allows you to kill it in the most humane way available at the time.

WHEN TO INFORM THE POLICE OR RSPCA

The police should be called if a farmer shoots a dog that has been worrying animals in their care, (see under Livestock earlier in this chapter). The police must also be informed if you suspect that an animal has entered the country illegally, or is being mistreated.

Under conservation laws it is illegal to release any animal that would not normally live in the countryside into the wild. These would include:

- coypu

- mink

- black rat

- grey squirrel

- prairie dog.

If after an accident the animal is still breathing and you cannot fairly ascertain whether or not it would be best to kill it then call the RSPCA. If the animal is small enough to be taken to the nearest known vet then you are allowed to leave the scene but let the police know as soon as reasonably possible. The vet's practice will not normally charge you for this if you mention that it was an accident and that the police are involved as the police have a fund to cover the vet's bills.

CASE STUDY

John gets bitten

John is out walking when for no reason he is bitten on the calf by a pit-bull terrier (classed as a dangerous dog). The owner, who John knows, is surprised as the dog has not bitten before, apologises at length and leaves. John correctly goes immediately to his nearest first aid point, a St Johns ambulance centre, where his wound is cleaned and dressed. The calf is tender for a while but causes no long-term effects. John decides not to sue for damages because he feels the man was being honest and when John had seen the dog before it had always looked placid.

John would have had trouble proving a claim because:

- The owner did genuinely believe the dog would not bite.

- The owner took responsible care of the animal.

- He would have had to prove the owner was negligent.

DISCUSSION POINTS

1. Should John have alerted the police in case the dog bites again?

2. What steps could the owner take to minimise the chance of it happening again?

3. Who should you call and how could you tell if an animal is being mistreated?

7

Food and Eating Out

THE LAW RELATING TO FOOD PREPARATION

The main regulations concerning food are the Food Safety (General Food Hygiene) Regulations 1995 and the Food Act 1984. The same regulations apply to all catering establishments, from a fast-food van, club, cafe, staff canteen to a top restaurant and also vending machines. During this chapter you may interpret 'restaurants' as any such eating establishment.

The only exceptions are:

- large fish markets
- dairies
- food produced by individuals which is donated to be sold in aid of voluntary organisations, registered charities, schools etc.

If food is transported away from the preparation site (marquee, fetes etc) then the containers should minimise pest infiltration, be suitable for the job and easily disinfected.

The law states that food must be supplied in a hygienic form and also comply with the description. There is no legal definition as to portion size unless a stated weight is mentioned. In practice this mainly applies to meat products (uncooked weight stated) and drinks. Bear in mind, however, that there is no minimum size of 'glass' so a glass of wine may well vary from establishment to establishment.

Obeying the rules

The proprietor must only obey the rules which apply. For example, you would not expect a fast-food van to have lavatorial facilities etc. The regulations allow the proprietor discretion but they must be inspected by the Environmental Health Department regularly.

Under the Weights and Measures Act there are separate regulations covering the actual amount of meat there must be in a meat pie (25 per cent), sausage (50 per cent) and so on and these are well policed. In all fairness manufacturers allow for this and it is rare to find a pre-packed food which does not comply.

The soft drinks industry also has its own regulations, the Soft Drinks Regulations 1964, which covers the amounts of fruit in fruit juice and so on.

In 1990 the Food Safety Law created a new approach which embraces many aspects of existing laws. With the arrival of 'E' numbers, GM foods and so on the law is constantly, being updated to consumers' benefit.

CONTAMINATED FOOD

The golden rule is to alert Trading Standards to any fault with any food or place where food is bought that you feel is wrong in any way. The Trading Standards office takes a strict line with persons convicted of selling food which does not comply with current regulations.

If you believe that the restaurant may not be complying with correct food preparation practices, with regard to the staff or premises, then your local Trading Standards office will look into your complaint on your behalf.

Legally food must be fit for human consumption and should not be tampered with to the detriment of the finished product. If you are served food from a packet or from individual wrappers then you can ask to see the packaging to check the 'sell by' and 'use by' dates. The difference between the two is fairly self-explanatory, but the storage conditions for each product will also have to be honoured.

There are however some food groups which do not have to be marked with such dates. They are:

- fresh fruit and vegetables

- wine, cider and any other drink apart from barley wine

- condensed and dried milk other than baby foods

- fruit juices

- sugar and certain chocolate confectionery

- coffee and coffee products

- any foods which keep for over 18 months without detriment to their quality.

Hygiene rules

All members of staff who handle food must ensure to the best of their ability that food is protected from becoming infected by obeying basic hygiene rules (such as separate cutting boards and knives for cooked and raw meat).

If you suspect that any rules have not been obeyed then you should report the matter to your local Environmental Health Department (housed at your local council).

LEVELS OF SERVICE YOU SHOULD EXPECT

As well as your legal rights you have the right to be treated with respect and spoken to politely and have any complaints dealt with in a fair manner.

Expectations you should have in respect to staffing are:

- Food must be delivered on clean crockery and all cutlery and glasses must be clean.

- All staff members must be aware of all food safety hazards.

- All surfaces which come into contact with food should be kept clean and in good repair.

- All staff members must know how to prevent food contamination.

- Catering managers must ensure all current safety controls are in place and operating efficiently.

- All clothing worn must be as clean as reasonably possible.

- All workers must maintain a high degree of personal cleanliness and work in a clean and hygienic way.

Food handlers must never smoke near food and must report any illness immediately to a superior (especially skin related disorders, diarrhoea and vomiting).

If they have a cut or an open wound they must wear a blue plaster (which is easily found if it becomes unstuck) or suitable dressings. They must also wash their hands frequently.

Management

You may believe that the problem lies more with the bad management of the premises than the staff. If for instance you notice that an egg just has rolled off a worktop onto the floor in the preparation area you should alert a member of staff. If however the same area is obviously very old and in bad repair you should direct a complaint to a member of management as it could be a health hazard. In the second scenario a telephone call to Trading Standards would be highly recommended.

Main regulations

Regulations state that all premises must:

- Be clean and in good repair.

- Have an adequate supply of drinking water.

- Have suitable protection to minimise pests.

- Have ample natural or artificial lighting and ventilation.

- Have suitable lavatories (with hot and cold water supply and suitable soap and drying equipment) which do not lead directly to food preparation rooms.

- Have adequate hand-washing facilities.

- Have adequate drainage and waste disposal systems.

ILLNESS FROM EATING CONTAMINATED FOOD

If you believe that eating food prepared from the site has caused you physical injury resulting in diarrhoea or vomiting, or has made you suspect you are the victim of food poisoning, then call your doctor immediately. They will probably want you to bring in a sample of your waste products for analysis. If you still have some of the uneaten food left over (scraps from a take-away or doggy bag) then it should be taken as soon as possible to Trading Standards who will analyse it for you.

If you can show that the restaurant was to blame you can issue a claim for compensation under a clause in the Sale of Goods Act 1979. If the restaurant is successfully prosecuted by the local authority (under the Food Act 1984) due to your alerting them of the problem, the court can order the restaurant to pay you compensation.

SERVICE CHARGES

If the service charge was covered in the price list displayed and the restaurant has provided you with good service, you are liable for this charge. If however you did not receive such service or the service charge was not obvious as part of the initial menu board, you do not have to pay it and hence you should deduct this charge from your bill.

WHEN TO DEMAND A REPLACEMENT MEAL/REDUCED BILL

There are situations where you may feel you have not been treated properly or the food portion size is inadequate. We often expect the measures in a restaurant or public house to match the quantities that we help ourselves to in our own home. Sometimes we are pleasantly surprised to find more, more often than not we find less. If you feel your meal is too small then politely ask for a bit extra and the manager will probably oblige.

Remember that as well as portion size the level and type of cooking may alter. You may usually have your carrots boiled for ages but this does not mean there is anything wrong with the steamed, slightly crunchy (yet still cooked) carrots served. Likewise you may find that your gin and tonic at the bar tastes weaker or your favourite bitter tastes different as it comes via a pump, not a can.

What you may class as inedible or undrinkable is palatable to others. If you have ordered an unfamiliar wine and it tastes horrid then in all fairness it is not the restaurant's fault. In such circumstances the regulations may become vague because of the grey area created by personal preferences. You are legally entitled to either refuse to pay, demand a replacement meal or state a reduction in your bill if:

- The meal was obviously inedible.
- The drinks were undrinkable.

- You were not served what you ordered (yet only discovered this after eating the meal).

- Portion sizes were obviously inadequate.

- The meal was not as described.

Which level of action to take will depend on the individual circumstances. If the meal has been partially or wholly eaten you can still complain about any aspect of it you were not happy with, but you must pay a reasonable amount for what you have eaten.

If you feel a reduction in the bill is appropriate then explain to the manager your reasons for requesting a reduction:

- Deduct what you think is a fair sum from the total.

- Inform the manager of your name and address.

- If the manager disagrees they have the option to sue you for the deduction.

As it could be very difficult for the manager to prove all your points were false the option of the restaurant taking legal action is rarely used.

Do not be put off by threats from the manager to call the police. Instead say this is fine as you can ask their advice on the laws relating to restaurants, witness the problem (mention that this might be useful in case it progresses to court) and advise as to whether any bill should be payable at all.

THE PRICE LIST EXPLAINED

There must be an easily-read menu that a prospective customer can see before entering. In self-service or fast-food restaurants the prices must also be at the food counter. In licensed restaurants selling wine a full wine list does not have to be shown, but they must show some examples from it so that the prospective customer is alerted to the likely expenses involved.

All menus must show, with reasonable equal provenance:

- the full price, inclusive of VAT

- any minimum charges

- any service charges.

Foods sold as home-made

If you suspect that a food advertised as home-made is in fact out of a can then complain immediately. A restaurant must comply with stated descriptions on the menu or from a waiter.

Sorry, that's off tonight

A restaurant does not have to have everything available on the menu. If you think the restaurant is genuinely trying to mislead customers, inform your local Trading Standards office.

Booked tables

If you have booked a table for a certain date and time then the restaurant must try their best to honour this. Sometimes the restaurant may have had particularly slow diners at a table which they expected would become vacant ready for your group. If you have arrived early then it would not be fair to expect the restaurant to find you a table straight away and you should allow for a slight delay up to and beyond your booked time.

If you feel that your delay will be too long then inform the manager that you and your party will be leaving shortly unless you can be seated. It is often useful to specify a time when your party will leave if they cannot be accommodated. If the restaurant cannot seat you then you can claim back a small sum for inconvenience and also reclaim your travel expenses.

If you discover that you will not be needing a table which had been booked then contact the restaurant as soon as possible. A restaurant can charge for a booked table if your party arrives late or is of a diminished size. It can however only charge for likely profits lost and not the full cost of the meal.

Paying by credit card

Check that the credit card is acceptable to the restaurant (most have signs displayed). By law restaurants do not have to accept credit cards or even cheques without prior consent. If your credit card is returned to you because it has been refused you should pay in cash or cheque or call the credit card company and ask for help. Most restaurants are willing to help as they would like to be paid.

Dress code and behaviour

A restaurant can refuse to serve you if you are not suitably dressed or acting in a manner which would disturb other diners. It does not matter if a table was pre-booked.

CASE STUDY

John's quarter-pounder is a five-pounder

A quarter-pound burger, chips and a large milkshake would just go down right, thinks John as he wanders into his favourite fast-food restaurant. The new management has kept the old staff and all seems well.

Settling down in his usual window seat John is soon served by a familiar and ever-helpful waitress and only has a short wait until his food arrives. He is familiar with the old menu and knows that he can have a meal here for under £4.

However when the bill is presented the cost is £9 with a charge of £5 alone for the burger. John is amazed and questions this with the waitress who produces a new menu off a nearby table, with price listings and service charge details. She points out a clear price list in a display case mounted onto the entrance doors and clearly readable from the outside.

John pays for the meal, along with a small service charge and considers complaining to the new manager.

John would have had difficulty making any valid complaint because:

- The new owner did not have to keep the old prices.

- The service charges were clearly stated on the menu and he had been served well by the waitress.

- The food was edible, as described and a fair portion.

- The drink was drinkable.

DISCUSSION POINTS

1. Should the management have made sure John had realised the price increases before letting him order?

2. Could John have deducted anything from the price charged?

3. What should John do now?

8

Property

YOUR LEGAL RIGHTS EXPLAINED

There is no legal obligation to insure your buildings or possessions, but if a mortgage is in place the lenders will insist on at least buildings insurance.

VANDALISM

Sometimes referred to as 'criminal damage'. It is an offence to destroy or damage property either intentionally or via recklessness.

LANDOWNERS' RIGHTS REGARDING TRESPASSERS

It is wrongly believed that trespassing is a criminal offence. It is in fact a civil offence and so signs 'trespassers will be prosecuted' actually carry no legal weight at all. Trespassers can be removed by the landowner with reasonable force depending on the situation but cannot be prosecuted just for being on the land. The landowner can take out an injunction against a regular trespasser which would mean it would then become illegal for them to continue trespassing, or risk being fined or even imprisoned.

Generally anyone can walk onto appropriate areas of your property unless there is a sign stating they are not welcome. So if a sign on the front gate states 'no salespersons welcome' then any salespersons coming onto the site are trespassers. Likewise a sign 'private property – keep out' would exclude any uninvited persons. What areas are suitable for certain persons would depend on the circumstances. The postman has an implied consent to walk to your letterbox and back but not to enter your shed (unless previously agreed with the owner that the shed is a suitable place to leave parcels when the house is empty).

Rights of way

It is illegal for a landowner to prevent the passage of persons using a public footpath, or riding a horse on a public bridleway. The rights involved are quite complicated but once a right of way has been created it is almost impossible for the landowner to re-acquire it. The main stipulation is that the right of way has been used for 20 years or over. If a landowner does not mind passage over the site, but wants to protect his position, then all he need do is close the path off for one day a year or via a formal notice deposited with the local council.

When trespassers can sue the landowner

A trespasser can sue the landowner for damages if they are injured intentionally whilst being evicted. If a trespasser enters ground that the owner knows to be dangerous and becomes injured then the landowner can also be sued. The fact that the trespasser should not have been there in the first place holds no legal standing.

A landowner cannot endanger the well-being of trespassers. Rail companies, building sites, poisonous areas, firing ranges and so on all have to have safety fences and signs to warn the public, even though they should not be on the site in the first place.

When landowners can sue the trespasser

Trespassers can be sued for any damage they cause whilst on the property.

To pursue any action you must be able to show that whoever trespassed had no implied consent. Every landowner has the right to protect their property using reasonable steps, but not to install hidden devices to injure those who trespass. A barbed or razor wire fence, non-drying security dye on tops of fences and so on are all acceptable. If you are unsure of what measures are appropriate call your crime prevention officer at the police station for advice.

ACCIDENTAL DAMAGE BY A CONTRACTOR

If a contractor or sub-contractor causes injury or damages property then whoever caused the damage is liable for the costs in rectifying the situation. Larger firms are usually better insured against this type of incident; some smaller contractors may operate with much less protection. If there is a secondary effect caused by a failure of a job because the work itself was not of good workmanship then you can also claim for this.

Example
Mr Pipe is having a new pump fitted to his gas central heating boiler by Mr Leeks plumbing co. All seems well and Mr Pipe and Mr Leek are chatting away whilst the work is being done. After completion all seems well but then a small flame appears off a gas pipe and scorches a kitchen unit. Mr Pipe is not very pleased when Mr Leek blames the pipe manufacturer.

Mr Pipe can claim for the cost and fitting of a new unit and a small amount for inconvenience caused. Mr Leek can try to claim the costs back from the pipe manufacturer.

YOUR HOME INSURANCE EXPLAINED

All home owners should have current insurance policies to cover buildings, contents and third party cover.

Insurance companies will not cover the full replacement costs of old, worn out contents or for damage caused where the main cause was lack of maintenance or vandalism by the insured.

Bear in mind that certain insurance companies offer a multitude of cover levels. It is wise to note details of what each insurance company is offering, and at what price, to ensure you get the cover you want. Almost all insurance companies are contactable on freephone numbers or via a broker.

Standard questions asked by insurance companies:

• Are all downstairs windows lockable?

• What type of locks do your external doors have (many insurers insist on a minimum five-lever deadlock)?

• Details of any intruder alarm if appropriate.

• Details of all previous claims made within five years.

• Details of any valuables.

• Details of any convictions or prosecutions pending for any persons living at the address.

• Estimate of building costs (knock down, take away rubble,

rebuild) – they should help you work this out (the Association of Insurance Brokers have a leaflet explaining this more fully).

- Value of contents, new replacement costs. Survey your home, not forgetting clothing, carpets, jewellery and so on. Add on 20 per cent for safety.

Valuable possessions

Insurance companies will need to be informed about possessions which you feel are valuable. In this case an 'item' may also include collections of smaller items such as stamps, medals and so on. It is essential to state the full worth of items you feel are valuable and ask for full coverage to that value. Some policies are worded in such a way as to limit the claim on a valuable object to a percentage of the total claim. The insurers may also ask for a valuation in writing from a suitably qualified source.

Any valuation figures should be supported by a written valuation from an appropriate expert source. It is always advisable to take pictures of any valuables in your home. Digital photography images could be downloaded onto a disc which could be kept in the bank or another safe place. This avoids the cost of processing and is highly recommended.

The information given will enable the insurer to work out their figures. If they discover that you have given false information they may declare the policy null and void. This would then mean you would have to shoulder the cost of any claim yourself. The police may also be involved as it is illegal to mislead and therefore tantamount to fraud.

Building, contents and third party cover

The only claim possibility which is appropriate to either type of policy is for third party claims made against the policy holder. This is normally covered by household insurance but can be requested if only building insurance is required.

Buildings and contents are often linked together by insurance companies but they are separate areas and can be insured separately.

Contents

This type of policy covers the policyholder against claims made for loss or damage to possessions which are located in the home and outbuildings.

Buildings
This covers essential damage to the building itself, as opposed to items held within it. The odd exemption is satellite dishes which for some reason are designated as contents.

Such areas covered would however include:

- chimney pots

- windows

- roofs and guttering

- outbuilding doors

- kitchen units

- floor tiles

- bathroom fittings

What's covered?
Damage of this type is usually caused by adverse weather conditions, fire or leaks from plumbing systems. If the type of mishap would involve claiming under both buildings and contents, such as the water from a burst pipe causing damage to a stereo, then the insurance company should advise. It is normal practice for insurance companies to have one form which covers both areas. If property is damaged by fire and further damage is caused by emergency services then this additional damage will also be covered. If the building was damaged by faulty workmanship you will be expected to sue the contractor for damage and loss and hence this type of claim is rejected.

Who can be insured?
Certain properties may be refused insurance. They may be of unusual construction or in a subsidence area. The insurance companies have lists of postcodes which have had problems with subsidence and have appropriate clauses regarding this. It is at the insurance company's discretion whether to impose certain restrictions in these situations.

Third party
This is the type of cover which is rarely claimed upon but can often be the most costly per claim. Like car insurance it is

to protect you from claims made against you for injury caused to another person.

It is not uncommon for a guest to suffer an injury in your house, be it from tripping over a child's toy or having an object fall on them. Not everyone is always covered under this type of policy. Family and friends may be excluded so check your policy documents if this is required. The reasoning behind this is that it is tempting to claim for an injury to a relation or friend as the policyholder's insurance company, not the insured person, would have to settle. The onus would be on the insurers to show the injured party and the insured were forging the claim. As the insured maximum amount is one million pounds the temptation can be large. If you are being sued for such a claim the insurance company will normally cover all legal costs for your defence, after all it is their money which is at stake. Remember that false claims are illegal and the insurance company could inform the police if they suspect the claim to not be true.

Three types of policy – starting with the cheapest

Indemnity
This type of policy would provide cover to restore a building or household item to its previous state, effectively taking into account wear and tear. Often the amount provided by insurers is not enough to cover the full cost of rectification.

Example
A television set which is five years old is damaged beyond repair after having a drink knocked over it during a party. The insurance company would take the cost of a new set, deduct quite a margin for wear and tear and forward the difference, less any excess, to the insured. The figures may resemble:

- new television £500

- deduction for wear and tear £300

- deduction of policy excess £150

- amount payable to insured £50.

The policyholder would have to find any extra funds in order to replace the set.

New-for-old
This is basically the same as an indemnity policy but with no deduction for wear and tear on some, but not all, items. However if the insurance company feels the policyholder was partly to blame (damage to possession because of poor maintenance, botched home repair etc) then a deduction may be made. Some insurers impose an age limit on certain items, after which a lower figure could be offered.

All risks
This is essentially the same as new-for-old but with the added protection of items that are taken out of the home such as cash, cameras, jewellery and so on. There is usually a maximum amount covered per claim, hence it is not recommended to take very valuable goods out of the home in multiples without checking your limits.

MAKING A CLAIM ON AN INSURANCE POLICY

Each type of situation requires its own type of remedial action. This could mean your initial phone call should be to the police, insurance company, ambulance service and so on.

You should inform your insurance company as soon as possible. They will probably have a specialist team to handle the claim and have assigned contractors who can minimise further problems with urgency, from repairing a burst pipe to making a house secure after a break-in.

* Remember that making a false claim is a criminal offence.

When assessing your claim the insurance company will apply the principle that you must not actually benefit from misfortune but only be put back into the situation you were in before the accident.

Remember the insurance premium will be based on the value of the goods. If you purchased a new computer for £2,000 three years ago, which is now worth £500, then £500 is the most you will get back if it is stolen or damaged beyond repair. It would be foolish to pay the premium based on £2,000.

The loss adjuster

The insurance company has the right to send a professional loss adjuster to evaluate the value of the claim. This is generally applicable if the claim is quite large. They will prepare a report for the insurance company and act independently. If you feel that the report is unfair you can instruct another loss adjuster, working for you, to prepare another claim. You will not be able to claim the cost of this second opinion from the insurers so this may be a false economy. Loss adjusters can be found in the *Yellow Pages* under 'Insurance Services & Administration' and should be able to give you an estimate of their costs.

The settlement

On settlement of the claim you may be asked to sign a letter of discharge which gives the impression that no more money can be claimed at a later date. If you later discover that you could have claimed more then re-pursue the matter. Most companies will reconsider any fair claim, regardless of the time differential.

If you genuinely feel that you have been mishandled by your insurance company, report the matter to the Insurance Ombudsman Bureau and the Association of British Insurers. You may feel that you will be better served by the Personal Insurance Arbitration Service which has an impartial approach. However, the decision reached is binding on both sides so advice on whether you would benefit should be taken beforehand.

Sometimes the compensation payable on a valuable object may be part of a maximum percentage allowance. The clause 'no individual item is to be worth more than 5% of total contents value' or words to that effect sometimes appears. If you have any valuable items worth over such a percentage, or over a set amount set by the insurance company, you should ensure they are listed on your confirmation of details sheet from your insurers (see Figure 6).

Example

Mrs Gogh has insurance which has a valuable item ceiling of 5 per cent of total insurance cover. In Mrs Gogh's house is a painting worth £5,000. The value of the rest of her possessions bring the total amount to £20,000. If a burglary occurs the 5 per cent rule would apply. Mrs Gogh's painting would be assessed at 5 per cent of £20,000 and she would only receive £1,000 compensation.

A.B.C Insurance Co

A.B.C House, 11 Damage Street, Anytown
Claims Tel No 0181 111 1111

Mr R U Insured
1 Blogs Street
Anytown ANY1 TN2

Date of loss	01 04 200X	*Policyholder's details*
When loss discovered	02 04 200X	Name – Mr Rob Unwin Insured
By whom	Spouse	Number – 111 1234 5678
Police notified	No	Address – 1 Blogs Street
Date police called	N/A	Anytown
Premises empty	No	ANY1 TN2
Furnished	Yes	Date of Birth – 01 01 1980
Is property let?	No	Occupation – Welder
Any other insurance	No	Tel – 0101 555 888

History of previous claims	*Date*	*Amount*
Storm damage	01 05 1998	£300

Details of previous convictions   None

How did loss occur?
Child spilled orange juice over back of TV set whilst having a children's party.

Details of claim
(please attach detailed estimate, valuation and evidence of value if appropriate)
Child knocked drink over set, set made a strange noise and then died.
TV Repair Co say circuit has been damaged (repair estimate enclosed).

Notes
Insurers and their agents share information to prevent false claims. These are based on terms listed in the Claims and Underwriting Register. The above claim will be provided to future agents and companies.

Declaration
I declare that the details are correct to the best of my knowledge and will assist the company further if required. I understand that you may seek information from previous insurers.

Policyholder's signature . . . .   **Date** . . . .

Fig. 6.   Sample of household insurance claim form.

CASE STUDY

The cards are stacked in John's favour

After a storm John's chimney stack is leaning badly. He calls the insurance company and they promptly send a builder to assess the damage. The builder says the stack must be removed and replaced (if appropriate).

John decides that he does not need the stack as he has central heating. The insurance company sends a loss adjuster to evaluate the damage and fill in appropriate forms. However he states that the stack must have been poorly maintained in order to suffer storm damage and instructs the insurance company to nullify the claim. John is not impressed and calls in his own loss adjuster who states the stack was in perfectly acceptable condition and the claim should stand. After consideration the insurance company pays for the removal of the stack and repair to the roof.

John was successful in this action because he:

- Alerted the insurance company quickly.

- Questioned, via an expert, a wrong judgment from the first adjuster sent by the insurance company.

- Had sufficient cover on his insurance policy.

DISCUSSION POINTS

1. Would the fact that the initial loss adjuster was contracted by the insurers have influenced his decision in favour of the insurance company?

2. Should John be able to claim the fee of the second adjuster back from his insurers?

3. In what other type of situation would the insurers send a loss adjuster to evaluate the claim?

9

Holidays

GENERAL ADVICE

Assuming the holiday destination is outside the UK there are basic steps which can be taken to minimise problems.

If you are planning to book a holiday it may be worth checking the internet. Many of the top tour operators now have internet sites. Holidays, flights, hotel reservations, flight schedules, car hire and other services can be booked on line, in real time.

The main sites are:

- www.expedia.com

- www.travelocity.com

- www.co-op-travelcare.co.uk

- www.city.net

- www.previewtravel.com

- www.thomascook.co.uk

Sometimes unsold tickets are auctioned off by the airlines and can be a good option for travellers who can leave promptly. If this appeals to you the main site menu includes:

- www.lufthansa.co.uk

- www.iflybritishmidland.com

- www.virgin-express.com

- www.lastminute.com

- www.holiday-retails.co.uk

Although on-line booking is considered safe it is not recommended that you give credit card details over the net or email unless you card is covered for internet fraud, and even then be very careful.

When you book a holiday with a travel agent or tour operator a contract is formed. Conditions stated on the booking form may not be enforceable if they can be shown to be unfair. If a travel agent causes loss or damage through negligence they can be claimed against.

Before you go

- Always book with a travel agent who has ABTA (Association of British Travel Agents) or ATOL (Air Travel Organisation Licence) membership.

- Arrange to take the majority of spending money in travellers' cheques as opposed to cash (the travellers' cheques may be insured). Check with your credit card company or bank for details.

- Look around for the best charges for conversion. There are often quite surprising differences between banks and bureaux de change, and between high street and airport.

- Inform police, milkman, postman, relations.

- Valuables may be left in a bank for a nominal charge.

- Check no final demands for bills may arrive whilst you are away, the last thing you want on your return is to find you have 'further action' being taken against you.

Whilst you're there

- Buy major foreign goods with a credit card as the card company may be jointly liable for future claims.

- Never keep your pin number with your credit card.

- Never keep your cheque book and guarantee card together.

- Only withdraw a small amount of cash at a time.

- Don't be afraid to haggle, many traders expect this and see tourists as an easy target.

If you have trouble remembering numbers then note it as a phone number, area code etc in your wallet/purse. That way if it is stolen the thief will not be sure of your pin code. Some card companies will let you pick your own number.

IATA, ABTA, ECR, E111 – WHAT IT ALL MEANS TO YOU

International Air Transport Association (IATA)

If the airline goes out of business whilst abroad, and you have booked through a travel agent, they must arrange for your return via an alternative airline. If you did not book with a travel agent you should approach another airline and ask if you can return on their aircraft, using the failed airlines ticket. This sounds odd but almost all airlines are members of IATA and will usually accept the tickets.

Association of British Travel Agents (ABTA)

ABTA administers help to anyone who has booked through one of their members. This would include services like making sure your tickets arrive on time, arranging flights and so on. If your travel agent goes into liquidation and was an ABTA member, they take over the responsibilities of that travel agent and will offer a refund or travel through a different tour operator.

Under the ABTA rules all members must:

- Advise prospective travellers about passports, inoculations and possible health problems.

- Ensure all booking agreements are easily understood and legible.

- Ensure booking agreements are fair and do not try to absolve the agent or operator against any chance of a future claim.

- Offer alternative travel arrangements or a refund if a holiday has to be cancelled by the agent or operator.

- Ensure all situations regarding surcharges are clearly shown in the brochure.

European Community Package Travel Regulations 1992 (ECR)

This is a little known Act which binds the travel companies in several ways. If you are claiming for holiday compensation then it may be worth finding this Act and quoting it with your claim (your local library should be able to help obtain a copy). If any problems arise with your holiday which you feel are worth claiming for then correct records will be essential. You should maximise your chances of compensation by:

- Keeping all receipts for any additional costs incurred.

- Noting problems with views, room etc (a photograph or video recording is always useful).

- Mentioning and noting all problems to the holiday rep and filling in an official complaint form (you should get a copy of each form).

- Mentioning the above Act when writing to the company involved.

E111
Fill in form E111 from the post office and check passport validity date. The Department of Health publishes a leaflet entitled Medical Costs Abroad which will advise you on what level of insurance you will need.

WHAT LEVEL OF SERVICE TO EXPECT

You should expect to be treated with fairness at all times and should receive the level of comfort implied in the brochures. If your accommodation is well below the standard expected, the hotel room not as described (sea view etc) or there has been a sudden change of hotel, you should complain to your holiday representative as soon as possible and note all things you are not happy with. Photos are always useful. Remember that this was part of the booking agreement, hence a breach of contract, and you are perfectly entitled to claim compensation or sue for loss of enjoyment and comfort.

You should expect that all the conditions listed in the ABTA code are abided by and that the agent informs you of any changes as soon as possible.

IF YOU FALL ILL ABROAD

If you fall ill or have an accident abroad which requires medical treatment you may sometimes have to pay for the treatment received and claim this back on your return. Forms SA30 and E111 cover these points. Each country has its own separate rules, some requiring just a passport for full coverage. Others have an arrangement where you will only be partially refunded costs under an E111. Check also that the cost of alternative travel arrangements, or the cost of return travel with a medical team, are covered under travel insurance.

If you are faced with a bill for treatment and do not have enough money then contact your own bank, credit card company or British consulate.

The leaflet SE30 explains all these combinations which, because of European politics, are subject to change quite quickly. The leaflet is available from your local department of health. The E111 is easily available from major post offices and should be taken on holiday with you in case it is required quickly.

COMMON PROBLEMS AND HOW TO RESOLVE THEM

Lost cases
If the airline loses your case you will need to fill in a Property Irregularity Report. The airline has a duty to supply you with funds to replace essential items as soon as a claim is made. You should claim against your holiday insurance for the rest of the items as soon as possible, obviously omitting the items already compensated for.

Plane was overbooked
Sometimes an airline issues too many tickets for air travel in case of 'no-shows'. If this happens the airline must give you cash compensation. The ECR sets compensation figures and appropriate guidelines for the airlines with larger awards for flights over 3,500km.

These figures are halved if the airline gets you to your destination within a delay of two hours.

What happens if I miss my plane?
Go immediately to the airline's check-in desk for help. They may put you on the next available flight or may arrange for another airline to transport you.

Holiday flight is held up through bad weather
The travel company should provide refreshments and if necessary an overnight stay. As the delay is not the fault of the operator then it is unlikely that any compensation is due but it may be worth checking the insurance package.

How much compensation should be claimed?

You need to break your figure into four separate sections and then total the amounts. State these workings when applying for compensation.

- Loss of value, if the hotel is more expensive what the extra cost is.

- If the room is unsatisfactory for two days in the week claim 2/7 of cost and so on.

- Out of pocket expenses, what extra costs you incurred.

- Loss of pleasure, no set rules but try to be fair.

If customer has to cancel a holiday

In this situation the agent or operator would normally keep the deposit. If the holiday was paid in full prior to cancellation then they may keep a fee to cover their expenses. This amount varies between agents and operators.

If the chosen travel agent was not an ABTA member and has gone into liquidation whilst you were on holiday then you should contact the Air Travel Reserve Fund.

Financial help

If the traveller is on a low income or disabled then the local social services department may be able to offer a grant. Some have special arrangements and are generally helpful.

Holiday homes

If you are considering buying a holiday home then bear in mind that if a television is present you will need a second licence unless you can show only one set will be used at any one time. If renting a holiday home then the licence becomes your liability for the duration of the stay. You may have to pay capital gains tax on profit made when the home is sold. It is advisable to clarify which home is your main abode with your local Inland Revenue office.

HOLIDAY INSURANCE EXPLAINED

Check with your own house insurers as to their travel and health insurance. It is often much cheaper than using the travel company's insurance.

It is a good idea to take a photocopy of the insurance details with you (leave the original at home) so you know your rights whilst on holiday.

Pay with your credit card, then if the tour operator goes bust you can claim against your card company. Always make the slip out to the tour operator – not the travel agent.

TIMESHARE PROPERTIES

Timeshare contracts entitle the purchaser to a specified amount of time per year when they have free reign over the property. If you visit the same holiday destination every year then this may make financial sense.

Beware of persons trying to persuade you to attend a presentation of any type because they could be selling time share apartments. You usually meet these persons on holiday and they use many, often devious, reasons to persuade you to attend a presentation. If you are not interested then walk away.

CASE STUDY

John's got a ticket to ride

Things are starting to look up for John as he has just booked a wonderful holiday in the Mediterranean. However, things start to go wrong when he arrives at the airport and is told that his flight has been delayed indefinitely because of bad weather. John can see that there is a fair amount of fog around so prepares for a fair wait. After many hours there is no sign of the fog lifting and all flight departures have been delayed.

The tour operator offers to accommodate John and his fellow travellers in hotels for the night. The operator supplies meals and drinks to its fogbound customers and hopes to be able to fly them out tomorrow.

Tomorrow dawns, the fog has lifted and all seems well. Then the tour representative arrives and informs them that because of the backlog their flight will be on a rota. Flights depart all day long until it is John's turn to fly. His plane is being loaded with luggage when the pilot has to stop the plane. John and his passengers are informed that the fog has travelled all the way to his island destination and that the local airport has been closed.

A second night is passed in the hotel before John finally flies out to discover that a small piece of hand luggage containing bathroom effects has been lost and he has to replace the contents and bag. Upon his return he writes to the tour operator claiming back a percentage of his holiday cost.

John will not receive much compensation because:

- It was not the airline's fault that there was fog.

- The tour operator made efforts to accommodate their passengers whilst delayed.

- The only additional costs which John has incurred were for the lost luggage. This expense will be refunded by the tour operator.

DISCUSSION POINTS

1. What natural problems could be classed as 'acts of god'?

2. Should John be able to claim for the lost holiday time?

3. What would be a fair amount John could attempt to claim for inconvenience?

10

Making a Claim via Legal Action

GOING TO COURT

Going to court should always be the last option. You will not be looked on favourably if you have not given the other side a fair chance of rectifying the problem prior to making a claim.

The details listed in this chapter are for all courts in England and Wales but Scottish courts have slightly different rules.

If you have a disability the court service have a helpline on 0800 358 3506 (minicom 0191 478 1476). It is also worth contacting the customer services officer at your local court.

If you feel that you have exhausted your efforts and that the debt owed is worth the trouble of court action, write to the other party stating your intentions. State clearly all details and always give a date on which proceedings will be started unless the debt is paid. Allow 14 days to rectify the situation as the court will expect you to have given a fair time limit.

Making the decision

Before you make a claim you should consider the other party's position. It is a waste of further money to pursue a debt against someone who you know cannot afford to pay it or has no assets of value. Even if the court decides that your debt is valid, and gives judgment for you, the process of actually getting the money is not always straightforward.

To find out whether a person is bankrupt contact the Insolvency Service. To find out whether a company or person has any unpaid court orders against them contact the Registry Trust Ltd. (currently charge £4.50 per name).

For a personal injury claim get a professional assessment from your doctor as soon as possible. A document referred to as the 'pre-action protocol' lists the steps you must have taken before you issue your claim. Such claims are best handled by trained experts.

Where to obtain legal advice:

- solicitor
- Citizens Advice Bureau
- law centre
- household or motor insurance policies sometimes have a legal service attached as part of their cover.

HOW TO MAKE A CLAIM

You can start your claim in any county court by completing form N1 (look in phone book under Courts). The form comes with notes to aid completion. If you decide to proceed then make a document file in which to keep photocopies of all forms, letters received and letters sent. Make one file for yourself, one for the court and one for each defendant. The judge will then decide which 'track' your claim will take.

How much does it cost?

How much it costs to make a claim will depend on the value of the claim itself. If you are on certain benefits you may not have to pay. If the claim is disputed or denied then further fees may be payable. Different rates apply depending on the amount of your claim.

Interest

You are entitled to claim interest on any debt at a daily rate which equates to 8% per annum. To work out interest owed complete the following calculation.

Debt x 0.00022 x number of days = £ . . . .

If you want to claim interest you must write your claim as 'The claimant claims interest under section 69 of the County Courts Act 1984 at the rate of 8% per year, from . . . . to . . . . of £ . . . . and also interest at the same rate up to the date of judgment or earlier payment at a daily rate of £ . . . .' Fill in the gaps as appropriate.

WHEN THE CLAIM IS RECEIVED

Next the defendant will be sent a response pack via the post office. The pack will contain the forms they need to reply to your claim. If the post office cannot deliver them the court will let you know and court staff can inform you of alternative delivery methods.

Upon receipt of the pack the defendant will have three choices:

- ignore it
- admit part or all of the claim
- dispute part or all of the claim.

Whether the defendant is admitting or disputing the claim they may apply for an extension from 14 to 28 days using form N9 (includes time in postal system) which is in their response pack. If you have not heard within 14 days contact the court immediately, asking for judgment by default. Until the court hears from you the defendant's reply will take priority, even if it is received after 14 days have passed. If the claim was for an 'unspecified amount' their non-reply will be forwarded to a procedural judge who decides whether a court hearing is needed.

Ignore it
If it is ignored then judgment could be made in your favour without further notice, for the amount of the claim or if requested the court will decide the claim value for you. This would enter the defendant's name in the Register of County Court Judgments which is used by credit agencies as a reference point before issuing mortgages, loans and so on.

If the case is not defended the claim format is designed to allow you to enforce payment yourself, with no, or only one visit to court. You will have to take copies of all relevant documents and witness or experts statements. If you win the case then more time will be spent filling in more forms to enforce judgment.

Admit part or all of the claim
In this case the defendant informs the court of their intentions and sends/takes the money to you within 14 days of the date they received the pack. If cash is paid you should give a receipt. If they admit the claim but do not have the money they can ask for time to pay.

You will receive form N9A from the defendant which states how they intend to pay. If their offer is acceptable ask the court to enter judgment on admission. They must keep up payments if possible. If they don't the court can, at your request, enforce the order and as a final measure can even commandeer goods, sell them and send you a payment.

If they dispute the amount they must send the court the relevant forms (N9B and N9A) putting their case. If the payment schedule offered is not acceptable you must write to the court explaining why. A court officer will work out a new rate and both parties will be informed accordingly. If the new plan is also unacceptable you may ask a judge to review figures. Details on these options would be listed on form 205A which was given to you when the claim was filed.

Dispute part or all of the claim

If the claim is for a fixed amount and the defendant is an individual then your claim may be transferred to the defendant's local county court. Additional travel, fair accommodation charge and lost wages may be added to your claim by the court. They must send the court the relevant form (N9B or N9D) putting their case.

If you cannot solve the situation mutually you will need to go to court. Court staff will assist in filling in the forms and advise on court procedure (see Figures 7 and 8). They cannot give you legal advice.

The court will notify you when they hear from the defendant, and send two more forms and if appropriate a new area where the case will be heard. The main form (N150) is an allocation questionnaire. The details on this form will show the judge which 'track' your claim will take. The court will also send you yet another form, an N10 which gives details on:

- date defendant received form

- any change of name/address

- defendant's solicitors if acting on their behalf in returning details to court

- defendant's intentions over the debt.

WHAT TYPE OF COURT

After sweeping changes to the legal system in 1999 the whole court system was reorganised. All claims now have to be dealt with quickly and the terminology has moved away from 'courts' and become 'tracks'.

1. Plaintiff sends form N1 to court	2. Court sends form N205A to plaintiff	3. Court sends defendant a Defence Pack	4. Defendant can apply for a 14-day extension (N9)
5. Defendant ignores court	5. Defendant admits the claim	5. Defendant defends all of claim	5. Defendant defends part of claim
6. Plaintiff gives defendant 14 days to reply	6. Court sends form N9A to plaintiff	6. When court receives form N9 from defendant it will send plaintiff form N10	6. When court receives form N9 from defendant it will send plaintiff form N10
7. Plaintiff asks court to enter judgment	7. If acceptable or not ask court to enter judgment or work out a figure for you. Both these are covered by the lower half of form N205A given to plaintiff when claim was issued	7. Defendant` will send form N9B to court	7. Defendant will send forms N9A and N9B to court
8. Court sends defendant form N30 stating payment details	8. Court will either send form N30(1) to defendant or form N30(2) to both plaintiff and defendant	8. Court will send forms N150 and N152 to defendant and plaintiff (also possibly form N271 if change of court area)	8. Court will send form N255A and copies of forms N9A and N9B returned by the defendant to the plaintiff
	9. If court's figures are unacceptable ask for a review	9. Court staff will refer the case to a judge to decide which track is appropriate	9. Plaintiff accepts lower sum or files forms N150 and N152 and follows path shown in left column

If defendant does not pay you the money which the court say they must then the court will take no action unless you tell them to. In the case of non-payment file an 'enforcement of judgment' notice to the court.

Plaintiff = person claiming.   Defendant = person being claimed from.
Specified = sum set by plaintiff.   Unspecified = sum decided by court officer.

Fig. 7.   Claiming in the courts – specified amounts.

Steps 1 to 5 – as Figure 7. Then:			
6. Court gives defendant 14 days to respond	6. Court sends form N9A to plaintiff	6. When court receives form N9 from defendant it will send plaintiff form N10	6. When court receives form N9 from defendant it will send plaintiff form N10
7. If still no answer court will ask a judge to decide on a dispersal hearing or pass to the appropriate track	7. Court will work out a fair repayment scheme	7. Defendant will send form N9D to the court	7. Defendant will send form N9A and form N9 to the court
	8. Court will send defendant form N30(2) stating payment details	8. Court will send form N150 and N152 to defendant and plaintiff (also possibly form N271 if a change of court area)	8. Court will send plaintiff form N255A and copies of forms returned from the defendant
	9. If figure decided by court is too low then ask for review	9. Court staff will refer case to judge to decide which track will be appropriate	9. Court calculates payment plan and sends form N30(2) to defendant
If defendant does not pay you the money which the court say they must then the court will take no action unless you tell them to. In the case of non-payment file an 'enforcement of judgment' notice to the court.			

Fig. 8. Claiming in the courts – unspecified amounts.

Small Claims Track

(Sometimes referred to as The Small Claims Court). The modernised system employed by the county court for handling small claims is designed to be quick, easy and fast but is only for claims up to £5,000 (or £1,000 for personal injury or housing disrepair). If defended you may take someone to speak on your behalf. This person, be it spouse, relative, friend or whatever is referred to as a 'lay representative'.

You may need persons to attend court to support your claim, and you may have to incur charges from these persons but, if you win the case the court may add these charges on to your claim. Only persons who have a valid reason for attending will be included. The court itself is fairly informal and should not be feared.

Such persons could be:

- a doctor

- a mechanic

- a surveyor

- an accountant

- a witness

- an interpreter (if English is not the first language)

- any other type of professional.

You will be allowed to claim for the following:

- court fees

- up to £260 for legal advice

- up to £200 for an expert's opinion

- up to £50 per day for yourself and any witness who has lost earnings

- personal travel and overnight expenses.
  (figures as at October 1999)

If the hearing date set by the judge is not suitable then you should inform the court immediately. The judge will usually want to hold a preliminary hearing if they feel one of you has no chance or the case is likely to be complicated.

Fast Track and Multi-Track

These will usually lead to a trial in open court which the public can attend. If the claim is defended you will receive a questionnaire (N150) which you must send back within 14 days. The idea of this questionnaire is to get both parties talking and agreeing on dates and so on. It also gives both parties one last chance to sort it out before going to court.

If the case would normally be held in the Fast Track, and if both parties agree then it can be referred to the Small Claims Track, provided the judge permits it. Only use expert evidence after the judge has given permission, or you will have to pay all the expert's costs yourself.

The Fast Track is normally for claims between £5,000 to £15,000 and is designed to last a maximum of five hours. For claims over £15,000 the Multi-Track applies. Leaflet EX305 explains this more fully but these two tracks have complicated rules relating to various cases and should be left in the hands of legal experts. Some solicitors will take the case on a no-win, no-fee basis.

LEGAL TERMS EXPLAINED

- Litigant – person involved in court actions.

- Defendant – person you are claiming from.

- Issue – start.

- Bailiff – court official.

- Specified amount – an exact figure claimed by yourself.

- Unspecified amount – when you let the court decide the amount for you.

- Served with – received.

- Served on – sent to.

- Disclosure – giving the other party all the information you have.

Leaflet references and titles
EX301 – Making a Claim? Some Questions to Ask Yourself
EX302 – How to Make a Claim
EX303 – A Claim has been Made Against Me – What Should I Do?
EX304 – No Reply to my Claim Form – What Should I Do?
EX305 – The Fast Track and the Multi-Track
EX306 – The Defendant Disputes All or Part of My Claim
EX307 – The Small Claims Track
EX308 – The Defendant Admits My Claim – I Did Not Claim a Fixed Amount of Money
EX309 – The Defendant Admits My Claim – I Claimed a Fixed Amount of Money

See Figures 7 and 8 – Claiming from the courts.

CASE STUDY

John comes into the breach
John has been letting out his previous home with a local rental agency for five years. His tenants seemed fine and prompt payers. The tenants emigrated and the house remained unlet for three months.

John goes to the house to do some redecorating. When he inspects it he finds many serious faults which have been getting worse over a long period. The repairs take a month to complete at a cost of £500.

A solicitor examines John's case with the agency and finds that they have been in breach because they did not carry out inspections as verbally agreed with John at the outset. The agency denies that there was any such verbal agreement and refuses the claim. John issues proceedings via the small claims track for an unspecified amount.

He visits the local county court and starts his action. The claim is for:

• Refund of management fees.

• Three months lost let whilst empty.

• One month lost let whilst being repaired.

- £500 repair costs (this would normally be obtained via deposit or from tenants but their deposit was refunded and they cannot be found).

The letting agency is happy to travel to John's local county court which after listening to both sides of the matter decides in John's favour. He is awarded the lost rental, £500 and a proportion of the management fees back (as the inspections were only a part of the fees).

John was successful in this action because he:

- Was not afraid to take the matter to court.

- Obtained professional legal help.

- Was able to convince the judge that he had been the subject of a breach of contract.

DISCUSSION POINTS

1. Under tenancy agreements an allowance is made for 'wear and tear'. How could you tell if a property was neglected or just 'well used'?

2. Did John have any alternative than to issue proceedings?

3. As the claim was under £5,000 John would have to pay for his own legal help. If the judge decided John's claim was over £5,000 what change would occur in his case as regards professional fees – from either side?

11

Employment

All businesses must have an employers liability (compulsory insurance) certificate which must be displayed so that any employee can read it easily.

Remember that all employers have a responsibility not just to their employees and customers but also to site visitors and anyone else affected by their business. Health and Safety at Work regulations include a duty to carry out assessments of risk unless there are under five employees or the risk is controlled, insignificant or inappropriate.

Staff should be encouraged to point out any areas where they may feel an accident could occur or where the health and safety rules are not being abided by. The appropriate legislation is available from the Health and Safety Executive (HSE) or from major bookstores.

UNFAIR DISMISSAL

Employers have a right to expect employees to act in a way which does not incite other workers and generally behave themselves. These are obligations set out by common law and if an employee fails to conduct themselves properly after being suitably warned then dismissal usually follows. A dismissed employee is entitled to confirmation of the reason for dismissal within 14 days of losing their post.

Almost all employees who have completed two full years service, working over 16 hours per week, can apply to an industrial tribunal for compensation if they feel they have been unfairly dismissed. This also applies to part-timers if they have worked for over five years and even some home-workers. It is unfair for an employer to place employees on extended trial periods in order to attempt to evade a claim for unfair dismissal. Once an employee has been employed for two years they are protected unless the job normally takes over two years' training.

It will be up to the employer to argue that the reason behind the decision was valid and fair. If you suspect that you have been unfairly dismissed then the local Citizens Advice Bureau is an excellent starting point as they will be informed of all the clauses of which there are very many.

When you cannot claim
You cannot claim for unfair dismissal if you:

- Come to the end of a fixed term contract.

- Are fired with colleagues if the firm goes into liquidation.

- Resign.

- Are made redundant.

- Were dismissed for embezzlement, theft, divulging trade secrets or another serious offence.

- Did not heed a previous warning that a certain aspect of your behaviour was required to change, eg absenteeism.

- Were dismissed after the employer discovers that essential qualifications claimed were not actually held.

- Are dismissed because of a 'frustrated' contract.

- Failed to pass a required test/examination ('unless frustrated') which you were previously informed about on initial acceptance of the position.

(See Figure 9.)

'Frustrated' contract
This means that the contract has been terminated without either party being directly to blame. Generally when the employee cannot work for a prolonged period the main reasons are:

- illness or hospitalisation

- imprisonment

- employee loses essential qualifications or other licence which would be legally required to work.

Although jury service would technically frustrate a contract any employer who dismisses an employee for attending as a member

Group	a	persons of retirement age
	b	crown servants
	c	merchant seamen
	d	part-time workers (up to 16 hours)
	e	close relative of employer
	f	employee who regularly works abroad
	g	fixed term contracts of three months or less

Employee has right to	If they have worked for	Entitled group
Written Employment contract	13 weeks	a and e
Notice of dismissal	1 month	a and e
Written reasons for dismissal	6 months	a,b,c,e and g
Unfair dismissal claim started work before 1986	2 years (firm has under 20 employees)	b,c and e
Redundancy payments	2 years	c
Redundancy consultation	any time via trade union	a,b,e and d
Maternity pay	2 years and was employed for first 26 weeks of term	a,b,c, and e
Reclaiming post after childbirth	with 3 weeks advance notice of intended return; returned within 29 weeks of confinement (only if firm has over five employees)	a,b,c and e
Itemised pay statement	any time	a,b,e and g
Guaranteed pay on short time or lay-off	1 month and provided that no days lost due to refusing alternative task or trade dispute	a,b,c and e
Equal pay	any time	a,b,d,e and g
Payment on insolvency of employer	any time	a,b,c,e and g
To belong to a trade union	any time	a,b,c,d,e and g

Fig. 9. Exceptions to the normal employment regulations.

of a jury would be open to a valid claim for unfair dismissal and also for contempt of court.

If an employee dies then obviously the contract is frustrated. His or her estate can however stil pursue the deceased's claim for wages due, redundancy payments and ongoing unfair dismissal claim.

When you can claim
You can claim for unfair dismissal if you:

- Were subject to a breach of employment contract.

- Were not allowed to resume your job after maternity leave.

- Refuse an alternative employment opportunity because you were insufficiently trained.

- Were not given fair warning that if a certain aspect of your manner was not corrected then dismissal would follow (this only applies if a notice period is applicable).

- Were lowered from full-time to part-time work without your consent.

Apprenticeships
Different rules apply to apprentices than to normal employees, along with different legal terms. Even the term employer is replaced by 'master', training replaced by 'indentures' and so on. The regulations on this area are due for change so if this applies, the local Citizens Advice Bureau or employment agency should be contacted.

Redundancy payment
Large redundancy payments, sometimes referred to as 'golden handshakes', are mainly tax free but these limits change. If in doubt then contact your local tax office.

Maternity leave
Any woman who takes maternity leave can return to her previous job if suitable. During this period she should receive from the employer a percentage of her usual wages. Some women are not automatically entitled to return; if the company has less than five employees or the pregnant woman is a member of the police or armed forces then they could not file for unfair dismissal.

To qualify for job re-acceptance you need to be a full-time employee or a part-timer who has over five years' service.

You are legally entitled to return to work if:

- You were employed until the 26th week of term.

- You give your employer over three months' written notice of your intention to return to work after the leave period.

- You return to work with 29 weeks of the birth (giving your employer at least three weeks' notification of return date).

Dates should be flexible if medical problems occur.

CONTRACT OF EMPLOYMENT EXPLAINED

The Employment Protection Act 1978 states that an employer must furnish an employee with a contract of employment within 13 weeks of starting work, but there is no direct action taken against employers who do not comply. If an employer is unsure of what to put in a contract then form P1700A available from the DTI or ACAS is very useful.

Every legally employed person has a legally binding employment contract with their employer that defines their obligations to each other.

Written details do not initially need to be in writing. A verbal agreement such as 'Monday to Friday, 9 till 5, 4 weeks a year off with pay' is legally acceptable if the other party accepts.

However, under the Employment Protection Act 1978 employers must provide a written list of implied terms, though not the contract itself, within 13 weeks of work starting.

If a claim is brought against an employer who has not furnished their employee with a contract then the employee has more chance of succeeding in a claim for unfair or constructive dismissal.

Under the Employment Consolidation Act 1978 written particulars must include:

- names of employee and employer

- employment start date and job title

- pay calculation details

- pension scheme details

- the company's disciplinary rules and procedures
- working hours
- holiday entitlement and pay
- sick pay arrangements
- dismissal and voluntary leaving notice periods.

Occasionally all the details will be written in a letter of appointment and this then becomes the basis of a contract.
Other areas which may be listed include:

- job requirements
- the person under whom they are directly responsible
- the company's trade union representative
- fire and safety regulations.

HEALTH AND SAFETY AT WORK

Under the Health and Safety at Work Act 1974 employers must ensure, to the best of their ability, the health and safety of their workforce. In many of these laws the word 'suitable' appears with regularity and so clouds many issues. New laws are in force covering the percentage of disabled employees a company must employ.

Temperature, lighting and ventilation

The temperature in the workslace should be over 16 degrees centigrade if the employee is inactive and at least 13 degrees centigrade when physically active. In some circumstances these limits may be changed by alternative legislation. To ensure this employees must have easy access to thermometers.

There should be sufficient lighting to create a safe working environment and also emergency lighting where a sudden loss of light would create a risk to the employees.

Likewise there should be sufficient ventilation with a fresh air supply available either via a window or mechanical means.

Space and cleanliness

Work areas should have enough space to allow employees to move about with ease. The legislation states that there should be at least 11 cubic metres of space per employee (if the room is over 3 metres high the space above is not countable).

All work surfaces, walls, floors and furnishings should be kept reasonably clean for the appropriate type of environment.

Workstations and seating

Workstations must be suitable for their task and easy to vacate in emergencies. Seating must be designed with the comfort of the operator in mind and feet should be supported if they cannot touch the floor.

It is advisable for employers not to economise too harshly on seating and compromise the correct posture of their employees. The cost of a new chair and properly set out workstation will mean less employee days lost, and minimise the risk of successful future employee claims for negligence resulting in back or neck problems.

Safety

Working areas that pose specific dangers, such as staircases, uneven floors, roofs, loading bays and so on must have suitable safety measures to protect employees. These may range from fencing, non-slip flooring or handrails to having mesh roofs installed to prevent items falling onto them from above. If there is a chance that an employee may fall 2 metres or over then guard rails with a minimum height of 1.1 metres must be installed to protect them. Suitable protective workwear must be provided by the employer (unless employing outside contractors) and should be worn when appropriate.

Water and toilet facilities

There should be suitable water distribution points, either fed off mains or from an enclosed system. Toilet facilities must be available and they also must be kept reasonably clean, be reasonably lit and ventilated. All washing facilities must have hot and cold running water, soap and hand-drying arrangements in place. Men and women must have their own toilet arrangements unless each facility has a lockable door and is for use by one person at a time.

Eating and rest areas

Suitable eating areas must be available unless the normal work-place has a suitable space to lay out food. Seating must be provided but as this is only for reasonably short periods the chairs can be less sympathetic as regards posture. If a canteen is available there should be no obligation to purchase food in order to sit. If no hot food purchase point is reasonably near then there should be a facility (usually a microwave) for employees to warm their own food. Rest areas must also have suitable arrangements to protect non-smokers from discomfort and passive smoking caused by smokers.

If you are unfortunate enough to suffer an injury whilst at work then report it as soon as possible. You should be handed a form F2508. These forms are available from the Health and Safety Executive if required.

UNIONS

Every worker has a legal right to belong to any union which accepts their membership application. Anyone who is dismissed for joining a union or taking part in union activities can claim unfair dismissal. Certain persons working for the government are not allowed to become union members, including civil servants and military personnel.

If the union is recognised by the employer then it can:

- Request information regarding the company for collective bargaining.

- Receive advance warning of prospective redundancies.

- Receive time off work for its members and other representatives to perform their duties.

- Be consulted on occupational pension schemes.

The rules are not legally binding but an employer who does not comply may be reported to the Central Arbitration Committee (CAC) which has the power to fix employment terms and conditions of the employees.

In certain circumstances the employer cannot divulge information which is irrelevant to a negotiation, would concern national security, cause damage to the business or concerns an individual. Information need only be divulged to a union representative authorised to carry out bargaining.

Union representatives must be consulted if redundances of

over ten persons are planned and the proposed losses concern the union. This notice must be given at least 30 days before redundancy notices are issued. For over 100 losses the time limit expands to 90 days.

Closed shops
These are agreements between an employer and a particular union, requiring employees to belong to that union as a condition of employment. If a worker is dismissed for refusing to join the union they can apply to an industrial tribunal, and can sue both union and employer if it can be shown the dismissal was caused by union pressure on the employer.

REDUNDANCY RIGHTS

If a firm goes into liquidation ex-employees can claim redundancy but not unfair dismissal. They are also entitled to claim unpaid wages and a time allowance towards pension contributions. The claim should be submitted through the receiver or liquidator to the Department of Employment.

If a firm asks for voluntary redundancy applications and this seems attractive then you should ask the company to confirm that the relevant redundancy payments will be issued if the offer is taken up. Without this the employer could state that there was a resignation and avoid a redundancy payment.

An employee serving out redundancy notice may leave to go to another job without detriment to their existing redundancy claim as long as one week's notice is given and served. If the employer wants the full notice period to be served then they can serve a counter-notice which must be served in writing during the period of notice.

CASE STUDY

John delivers an ultimatum
John has been working as a delivery driver for a large parcel delivery service when he is called into his manager's office. He is told that because of staffing problems he is to work in the accounts department until further notice. John is totally bereft of any office skills and politely refuses to work there unless

he receives extra training because he would not feel competent.

The manager feels that John is being difficult and says that unless he moves to the accounts department he will be sacked for refusing to work as it can't be that hard to add up a few numbers. John goes to examine the accounts department to find out what the job entails and discovers a room full of modern computers, running very complicated-looking software. He explains his lack of computer skills and accounts knowledge to the department head who agrees that he cannot do the job. John returns to his manager, is sacked for refusing work and given detail of notice.

John visits his local Citizens Advice Bureau who assist him in a claim for unfair dismissal as he feels he has been treated unfairly. After consideration his manager backs down and informs John that he has spoken with the accounts department and did not realise how complicated the job was. John is reinstated but manages to convince his employer to cover the cost of paid college classes (within company time) so that he is sufficiently trained in case the situation reoccurs.

John was successful in this action because he:

- Stated his reason for declining the post.

- Visited the accounts department to see if the job was manageable.

- Managed to get the employer to pay for training, which will come in useful in case of internal transfer within the company or for his next employer.

DISCUSSION POINTS

1. Is it always so obvious that a new job is unsuitable?

2. Could John have claimed for unfair dismissal if he had resigned without giving any reason for job refusal?

3. A part-time worker can file for unfair dismissal after five years as opposed to two years for a full-time employee. Is this time difference reasonable or does it encourage employers to employ part-timers as opposed to full-time workers to limit the chance of a claim?

Glossary

AIB. Association of Insurance Brokers.

Assault. A violent attack, either physically or verbally (whether or not an actual injury is sustained). If contact is made after threatening verbal abuse then it becomes assault and battery.

By-law. Localised regulation imposed by local authority.

CICA. Criminal Injuries Compensation Authority. A government-funded compensation scheme for persons affected by criminal actions.

Claim. Retribution, usually with money, for dues owed to a person because of someone else's negligence.

Compensation. The amount that is claimed in order to make amends for what the other party has done.

Consulate. The building where a country's consul is based. The consul is an official appointed by their government to work in a foreign country and whose job is to protect their home country's citizens and interests.

Contractor. A person or company employed to perform a specific contract.

Council. The government department that deals with the day-to-day running of your area.

Credit agencies. Organisations that keep records of any personal financial problems. When a person applies for credit these agencies are contacted to determine whether you are a good risk.

De-trunked. When a road is transferred from control by the highways agency to the local council.

Disclaimer. A notice which has been erected in order to deter the public from taking any action against the owner or management of a site by stating that no claims can be made against them.

Drugs. Many are safe but illegal drugs are dangerous. If you think one has been used and is a contributory part of a claim then call the police immediately. The effects of drugs can be apparent drunkenness, drowsiness, extreme restlessness, flushed skin, hysterical outbursts, terror, twitching and a tendency to be violent.

DVLC. Driver and Vehicle Licensing Centre. Where information regarding vehicle ownership is kept.

DVLA. Driver and Vehicle Licensing Agency. Where details relating to driving licences and road fund licences (tax discs) are kept.

'E' numbers. The system used for listing additives in foods where each additive, preservative and colouring is given its own reference number.

Evidence. Proof of an occurrence which could be used to validate a claim.

GM (foods). Genetically modified foods are where the genetic code which determines the food's resistance to pests, etc has been modified using technology.

Judge. Person appointed to hear and decide upon cases brought into a court of justice.

Law centre. An independent advisory service, similar to the Citizens Advice Bureau but specialising in legal advice.

Liability. A person or item that has become troublesome and may become the main cause of a claim.

Liquidation. When a company is wound up its assets and liabilities are removed from current management and taken over by a group of receivers appointed by the institutions they owe money to.

Legislation. The process of law-making as set out by government.

Maladministration. Where the usual procedure of administration has failed through inefficiency, dishonesty or negligence and an administration error has occurred.

Nullify. When something is cancelled out, an event or claim erased or neutralised.

Ombudsman. A government official whose job is to investigate an individual's complaint against a public authority.

Real-time. Computer term which indicates that there is almost no delay in any information being sent between computers. Useful where a delay would cause problems. Examples include booking airline tickets, theatre tickets, shopping or auction bidding via computer.

Register of county court judgments. A register of persons who have been taken to court over a debt and where the judge has decided that they do owe the money. Sometimes referred to as CCJs (County Court Judgments).

Road fund licence. A fee paid to the government for use of the roads, indicated by the displaying of a tax disc.

Solicitor. A member of the legal profession who is qualified to assist in the drawing of wills, conveyancing, instruct barristers and represent clients in the majority of courts.

Timeshare. A system where a property is owned by several individuals who each have the use of the property for a certain period each year.

VAT. Value Added Tax.

Witness. A person who has seen an event and who will freely impart information on what they saw in order to support a claim.

Useful Addresses

Advisory, Concilliation & Arbitration Service (ACAS), Head Office, Barndon House, 180 Borough High Street, London SE1 1LW. Tel: (020) 7396 5100.

Air Travel Reserve Fund, 20 Manvers Street, Bath BA1 1LX.

Association of British Insurers, 51 Gresham Street London EC2V 7HQ.

Association of British Travel Agents (ABTA), 55–57 Newman Street, London W1P 4AH.

Banking Ombudsman, No 70, Grays Inn Road, London WC1 8NB.

Department of Trade & Industry (DTi), 1 Victoria Street, London SW1H 0ET. Tel: (020) 7215 5000. http://www.dti.gov.uk/

Health and Safety Executive – Books, PO Box 1999, Sudbury, Suffolk CO10 6FS.

Health and Safety Executive – Information, Information Centre, Broad Lane, Sheffield S3 7HQ.

Insolvency Service, 21 Bloomsbury Street, London WC1B 3SS. Tel (020) 7637 1110.

Insurance Ombudsman Bureau, City Gate One, 135 Part Street, London SE1 9EA.

Registry Trust Ltd, 173–175 Cleveland Street, London W1P 5PE. Tel: (020) 7380 0133.

Further Reading

English Law, Denis Keenan, (Pitman).
Guide to the Law, J. Pritchard (Penguin).
Right Guide for Home Owners, Jan Cuba and Derek McConnell, (Shac).
The Highway Code, (Stationery Office).
You and Your Rights, (Readers Digest).
Your Home and the Law, (Good Housekeeping Guide).

Index